# REEF CORAL
## Identification

### FLORIDA CARIBBEAN BAHAMAS
Including Marine Plants

# PAUL HUMANN

EDITED BY
## NED DELOACH

## NEW WORLD PUBLICATIONS, INC.

Printed by
**Paramount Miller Graphics, Inc.**
Jacksonville, Florida U.S.A.

# Acknowledgements

This book was the result of considerable encouragement, help, and advice from many friends and acquaintances. It became a much larger undertaking and involved many more people than ever expected. I wish to express my sincere gratitude to everyone involved. Naturally, the names of a few who played especially significant roles come to mind.

Mary DeLoach and Jackie Jones gave valuable assistance in the editing process. Joe Gies and Michael O'Connell were most helpful with advice and assistance in design, layout, typesetting and production. Finally, I must mention editor, friend and business partner Ned DeLoach, without whose help this project would never have been completed.

Long time friend Adrien Briggs, and the entire staff at Sunset House, Grand Cayman helped make our photographic trip to the islands most successful. Fellow underwater photographer Cathy Church and her staff kept my cameras working and provided important daily developing service. Diving companions Sol Fiser and Mike Bacon were indispensable assistants in finding many of the cryptic corals. Wonderful friends, John and Marion Bacon gave generously of their time, assistance, and boat, helping me photograph corals of East Florida. Captain Dan Morrison, Captain Julie Jordan and Jason Wesley of the Aggressor Fleet offered valuable assistance in finding uncommon species. Mark Ulmann's knowledge of northeast Florida's reefs was most valuable. Peter Hull and Gary Gilliland with Mote Marine Laboratory, in Sarasota, Florida, expedited my locating and photographing several species unique to West Florida.

**PHOTO CREDITS**

*Dr. Douglas Fenner* 19c, 20a, 21a, 145c; *Dr. Walter Jaap* 91c; *Mike Bacon* 193b, 195a, 213a, 215a, 226b; *Jeri Clark* 118a; *Ned DeLoach* 72b, 73a, 76c, 77b & c, 78b & c, 79a,b & c, 102, 103a & b, 190b; *Bryan Willy* 5; all other pictures were taken by the author, *Paul Humann*.

**CREDITS**

Editor: Ned DeLoach
Layout & Design: Paul Humann & Ned DeLoach
Art Direction, Drawings & Typography: Joe Gies & Michael O'Connell
Color Separations & Printing: Paramount Miller Graphics, Inc., Jacksonville, FL
First Printing: 1993. Revised Second Printing 1994. 3rd Printing 1996. Revised 4th Printing 1998.
ISBN 1-878348-03-5
Library of Congress applied for.
Copyright: ©1993 Paul Humann

Published and Distributed by New World Publications, Inc., Jacksonville, FL 32207 Phone (904) 737-6558

# Author's Note and Scientific Acknowledgements

Biological scientists that specialize in identifying, describing and classifying plants and animals according to their presumed natural relationships, are called taxonomists. Generally they are a rare breed because of the limited research money and grants and few positions available in museums and universities for their particular talents. In fact, for many world authorities taxonomy is more a hobby than a profession. Their job descriptions generally entail other studies such as biomedical research, reef surveys, commercial marine harvesting, ecological and environmental surveys, etc. One of my most pressing problems during the extended research for each volume of the *Reef Set* was finding taxonomists to help with the identification process. For instance, it was necessary to correspond with a retired scientist from the British Museum of Natural History to acquire information concerning flatworms for the *Reef Creature* text — there was no one in the United States who could help!

Biological research is based on accurate taxonomy, yet lack of funding for this discipline continues to be a problem. A recent example came to light in a 1992 paper by Nancy Knowlton, *et al*, who found evidence that Boulder Star Coral [pg. 112] commonly used as an indicator of reef health is probably four closely related but separate species with different growth rates and reactions to environmental changes. If her findings are correct, it means that the conclusions drawn from years of ecological and environmental reef research in Florida, the Bahamas and Caribbean may be invalid! The need for more basic taxonomy research is further emphasized by the eight scientifically undescribed species included in this book, not to mention the even larger number of described species that desperately need further study and possible reclassification.

Special tribute must be given to the numerous scientists who gave freely of their time, advice and knowledge. Each is a preeminent authority in his respective field, and without their most generous assistance, this book could have never been published. Every attempt was made to keep the text and identifications accurate. Where errors may exist, they are my sole responsibility.

The invaluable assistance of **Dr. Walter Goldberg**, of Florida International University, deserves special mention. He undertook the Herculean task as principal scientific advisor, and coordinator for this project. **Dr. Dennis Opresko** with the Oak Ridge National Laboratory assisted with black corals. **Dr. Dale Calder** from the Royal Ontario Museum offered advice on the fire corals. **Dr. David Ballantine**, Department of Marine Sciences, University of Puerto Rico advised and identified algae.

**Dr. Stephen Cairns** with the National Museum of Natural History, Smithsonian Institution was my primary mentor for stony corals. To substantiate the identifications of many species, small samples were collected of many photographed specimens and shipped to the Smithsonian for his examination. Those specimens were placed in the permanent National Collection and are indicated in this book by their "USNM" numbers. **Dr. Walter Jaap** with the Florida Marine Research Institute also assisted with stony corals, examining and identifying several collected specimens. **Dr. Douglas Fenner,** Australian Institute of Marine Science, has been a constant source of valuable information. He located a number of uncommon species, provided several pictures and was especially helpful in sorting out visual ID clues to similar appearing *Agaricia* species.

**Dr. Jennifer Wheaton** with the Florida Marine Research Institute was my primary advisor for octocorallians. Her knowledge from reef survey work was invaluable in establishing visual identification keys for many species. Dr. Goldberg made several dives with me to help sort out the mind boggling variety of octocorallians off Florida's east coast. In the laboratory he taught me how scientists reduce small slivers of gorgonian specimens to their structural spicules to determine their species by microscopic examination. Several difficult identification problems were forwarded to **Dr. Frederick Bayer,** the acknowledged world's octocorallian authority at the Smithsonian. Because of his help, the photographs of several living species were published in this book for the first time.

# Editor's Note

Corals flourish in warm, clear, shallow seas. Along the Florida Keys' Atlantic fringe, throughout the Bahamas' Island chain, and spreading south and west across the tropical waters of the Caribbean Sea, great coral reefs abound. Towering sea-sculptures adorned with waving gardens of flexible coral fans, whips and plumes provide sanctuary to one of our earth's most diverse and visually stunning ecosystems.

It has only been with our recent ability to freely explore this dramatic underwater wilderness that we are beginning to unravel its complex nature. Even with limited data, it is readily apparent that environmental changes both natural and unnatural have had a harsh impact on coral habitats. Oil spills, sewage, coastal development, overuse by watersportsmen, groundings, over-harvesting, global warming, El Niño, algal blooms, and storms: the list of culprits is long. Our lack of knowledge, however, is the reef's greatest threat.

An ancient Chinese proverb states: THE BEGINNING OF WISDOM IS GETTING THINGS BY THEIR RIGHT NAME. A single, healthy reef section may consist of over 50 coral species, but only a few divers are able to identify even the most common corals. The ability to recognize individual life forms on the reef is the critical distinction between an underwater sightseer and the underwater naturalist. The guardianship of the world's coral gardens should, by right, rest on the shoulders of the recreational diving community. But, we have yet to educate ourselves in order to make prudent decisions about the coral reef's protection and utilization.

For decades North American birdwatchers have been accumulating a wealth of data monitoring bird species. The enjoyable pastime has produced an invaluable resource for their environmental concerns. Comparable information about the reef's inhabitants remains unavailable even for areas that are visited by thousands of divers each year. It is imperative that the recreational diving community makes a similar commitment to marine life by taking an active role monitoring our coral reefs.

*Reef Coral Identification* is the first comprehensive photographic guide for the visual identification of corals and marine plants that inhabit the Florida, Caribbean and Bahama waters. It is designed to help recreational divers, as well as scientists, distinguish the many species of corals and algae encountered while exploring the reefs. This is the third text of a three volume set that includes *Reef Fish Identification* (1989), and *Reef Creature Identification* (1992).

It is the intent of author/photographer Paul Humann and the marine biologists that helped with this ambitious project that it serve as a catalyst for continued study, documentation, and preservation of our living coral habitants — the last natural history on our planet yet to unfold.

# About the Author

To find Paul Humann at his south Florida home, you have to cut through his dining room which is lined, wall and floor, with primitive art from jungle civilizations around the world. The large family room, no less impressively decorated, showcases fish, turtle and whale carvings — each created by island hands. A dazzling collection of his favorite Galapagos wildlife prints cover the left wall; a dozen fiercely-proud New Guinea tribesmen stare down from their tack-sharp portraits on the wall just to the right of the back door. Outside, a wooden deck, perpetually shaded by a towering mango tree, curves to the right under spreading limbs dripping with fern and orchid baskets, passes through a jungle of Australian fern trees and bromeliads, and ends abruptly before a nondescript aluminum storm door that opens into the unkempt garage/office of an extremely busy man.

Whenever Paul has been in the States during the past six years, he has been here. Early mornings to late evenings find him wedged in a pre-1970 K-Mart swivel chair that sits hopelessly trapped before the tireless glow of a computer screen by fallen reams of drafts, correspondence and, scientific publications. Steam from a stained mug filled with strong Ecuadorian brew edges up from amidst the clutter. On the unfinished plyboard table to his left two color-corrected slide viewing boxes, spread with an ocean of blue transparencies, illuminate listing shelves packed with a well-used marine life library. From a nail hangs a cheaply framed Juris Doctor degree — a relic from an almost forgotten time. The remainder of the 10 X 20 foot concrete floor supports cheap, metal shelving piled with various office supplies, darkroom equipment and an unplanned museum of underwater photography equipment. A few dust covered pieces date from mid-century — the embryonic era of underwater exploration. The only order found anywhere within the cavernous room is behind the thick, double doors of a large fire safe where carefully labeled and neatly stacked transparency storage cases hold the rich treasures from 30 years of bountiful underwater hunting with a camera.

Though Paul's photographic search for marine species started in the 1960's, it really began in earnest in 1971 when he left a successful law practice in his hometown Wichita, Kansas to buy and captain the now legendary *Cayman Diver* — the Caribbean's first successful live-aboard diving cruiser. This bold move offered the unique opportunity to dive daily with the exotic creatures of the Caribbean reef. Paul sold the yacht in 1979, gaining even more freedom to travel, write and explore the world's coral reefs.

Hard work, relentless study and the courage to follow his dream, has led to the publication of eight books, numerous magazine articles and the comprehensive three volume *Reef Set* — an unparalleled marine life identification reference heralded by the diving and scientific communities alike.

These pioneering efforts in marine life identification have required much more than the difficult task of capturing each species on film. Long hours of observation, as well as the painstaking collection, preservation, and shipment of photographed specimens to scientific mentors around the world, were crucial to establishing accurate identifications for hundreds of species.

Even with all his accomplishments, Paul has no intention of resting on past achievements. He continues to write and teach about marine life and gather information and photographs for future editions of the *Reef Set*. He does, however, plan to spend less time in his office and more time where he loves to be – traveling the world and exploring the endless wonders of the sea.

# Contents

## Ten Identification Groups
## Common & Proper Phylum Names

### 1. Hydrocorals 14-21

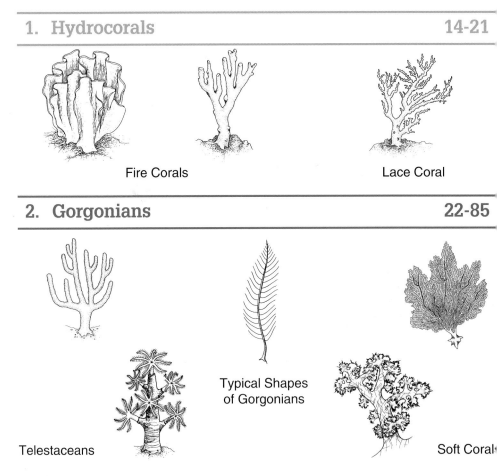

Fire Corals
Lace Coral

### 2. Gorgonians 22-85

Typical Shapes of Gorgonians

Telestaceans
Soft Coral

6

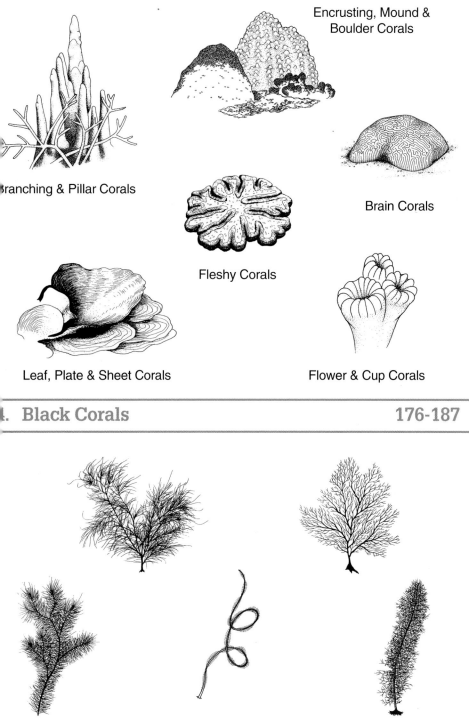

Encrusting, Mound &
Boulder Corals

Branching & Pillar Corals

Brain Corals

Fleshy Corals

Leaf, Plate & Sheet Corals

Flower & Cup Corals

# 4. Black Corals 176-187

Typical Shapes of Black Corals

# Overview

Corals are tiny animals that generally group together by the thousands, forming colonies that attach to hard surfaces of the sea floor. By drawing calcium carbonate from seawater they build skeletal structures in an infinite variety of shapes and sizes. Those species known as reef building corals, produce massive skeletons that collectively form the limestone framework of tropical reefs. Throughout the ages a vast array of animals and plants have become associated with coral reefs, creating some of our earth's most fascinating, complex and biologically diverse ecosystems.

All corals are members of the Animal Kingdom and classified in Phylum Cnidaria (Nigh-DARE-ee-uh/ L. a nettle [formally known as Phylum Coelenterata/L. open gut]). They are often mistaken for plants because of their attachment to the substrate, apparent lack of independent movement and superficial resemblance to flora. In fact, corals were classified as plants until 1753, when French biologists J.A. de Peysonell, making a study in the western Atlantic, concluded they were animals. Although corals are the best known cnidarians, the phylum also includes several other well-known groups including hydroids, jellyfish, and anemones.

Cnidarians have a simple anatomy consisting of a cup-shaped body, with a single, central opening that is encircled by tentacles. This opening functions both as a mouth and anus. Most phylum members attach their bodies to the substrate; in this form they are known as polyps. Polyps can live singly, such as most anemones, or they can reproduce asexually to form ever expanding colonies, which is typical of most corals. Noncolonial, unattached, free swimming members of the phylum are known as medusa or jellyfish. A unique characteristic shared by virtually all cnidarians is the presence of numerous stinging capsules, called nematocysts or cnidae, which is the origin of the phylum's Latin name. These minute capsules, located primarily on the tentacles, are used for both capturing prey and defense. With the exception of fire corals, the stings of most corals have no harmful effect on divers.

For coral reefs to develop, the delicate polyps must flourish. This requires several critical environmental factors, including: water temperature, movement, salinity, clarity, and a firm base for attachment. Water temperature must generally remain between 70 and 85 degrees Fahrenheit for the reef building colonies to grow. Species can survive below or above these points, but do not grow at a rate sufficient to construct reefs. Water movement sustains life by refreshing the supply of planktonic food and oxygen. Water clarity is also important. It allows the passage of light, essential for the growth of single-celled plants, called zooxanthellae (zo-zan-THEL-ee), that grow within the coral polyps' tissue. Zooxanthellae play a vital role in the polyps' ability to produce calcium carbonate for their skeletons. Reduced clarity, caused by settling silt particles, limits the polyps' ability to feed by literally choking them. Even under ideal conditions coral growth is slow, measuring less than an inch each year for most species.

In addition to the reef building corals this volume also includes the cnidarians commonly known as fire corals, lace corals, gorgonians (sometimes called soft corals) and black corals. All other cnidarians are identified in the companion volume,

*Reef Creature Identification.* Marine flowering plants and algae play a vital role in the reefs' ecosystems and are included as an appendix to this volume. Many of these species, known as coralline algae, also employ calcium carbonate to support their structure. In this way they contribute substantially to the reef building process by filling voids and actually cementing the reef's framework together.

# Types Of Coral Reefs, Structures And Terms

The basic types of coral reefs are generally defined by their overall structure and the geological conditions under which they evolved. These distinctions are sometimes obscure because of overlapping stages in the continuum of their development. Most marine scientists agree that there are three basic types of coral reefs and possibly five. In broad, idealized terms, the reef types may be described as follows:

**Fringing Reefs** grow out from the shore or are separated by a shallow lagoon. They generally parallel the coastline and at their shallowest often break or nearly reach the water's surface. They are common around most Caribbean and Bahamian islands, but are virtually absent along both Florida coasts and the Florida Keys. Geologically they are considered to be the youngest type of reef.

**Barrier Reefs** generally grow parallel to a coastline, but are separated by extensive distance and relatively deep lagoon. The distance may vary from about one mile to 25 miles or more and the lagoon often exceeds 60 feet in depth. At their shallowest they often break or nearly reach the water's surface, forming a "barrier" to navigation. The outer edge of a barrier reef drops from the island platform or continental shelf into very deep water. The best example in the Western Hemisphere is the world's second longest, skirting the small Central American country of Belize. Typically, fringing reefs change to barrier reefs when their associated land mass undergoes a slow geologic sinking.

**Atolls** are open sea reefs that form rings, ovals or horseshoe-shapes around a shallow lagoon. Occasionally small coral islands that may support vegetation form as a part of the ring. On the outside the fore reef drops into deep water. Atolls are generally found in the tropical Pacific where large geological plates supporting volcanic peaks gradually sink. Fringing reefs first form around the volcanic islands. As the plate sinks, the reefs become more distant from the land and grow upward, forming barrier reefs. The final stage of an atoll's development occurs when the volcanic island is completely submerged, leaving the lagoon in its place. There are a few atolls in the Western Atlantic, but they were not formed from submerging volcanos as in the Pacific. The best known are Lighthouse, Glovers' and Turneffe off Belize, Chinchirro off Yucatan and Hogsty in the Bahamas.

**Bank Reefs** are open sea reefs, without a central lagoon, surrounded by deep water and miles from any land mass. The Great Bahama Bank, Ten Mile Banks off Grand Cayman, and Serranilla Bank and Misteriosa Bank located in the Northwest Caribbean are-well known examples. Some scientists also describe the reefs off the Florida Keys as bank reefs, while others consider them as a combination of bank and barrier.

**Patch Reefs** are small, isolated reef areas that grow up from the open bottom of the island platform or continental shelf. They generally occur between the fringing reefs and barrier reef, if one is present. A patch reef may vary in size from a small house to an area that could cover several city blocks. Depths also vary greatly, but the reef's crest rarely breaks the surface.

**Coral Heads** are similar to patch reefs, but smaller in size. They are primarily formed by a single coral colony, such as a huge brain or star coral, but may include several smaller colonies of the same or different species.

**Reef Crest** is the top of a reef system.

**Back Reef** is the area behind fringing reefs, usually protected, calm and often containing a mosaic of shallow coral heads, patch reefs and turtle grass.

**Lagoon** is a relatively shallow, calm, protected area behind a fringing or barrier reef. It often includes great expanses of sand flats and grass beds and occasional coral heads.

**Fore Reef** is the area on the seaward side of any reef, but refers primarily to the portions that project into deeper water.

**Tongue & Groove** are long ridges separated by valleys of sand that generally run toward the direction of the prevailing swells. They often occur in shallow water near the reef crests, but may also be found on the fore reef. The ridges are also termed spurs or buttresses. The valleys are also called sand channels, sand chutes, and, if narrow with high, steep sides, canyons.

**Walls** are underwater cliffs that drop at or near a 90 degree angle. They are often associated with the outer limits of an island platform or continental shelf.

**Wall Lips** are ridges that often form and run along the upper edge of a wall. The ridge can be slight or over 20 to 30 feet in height.

# How To Use This Book

The animals in Phylum Cnidaria are classified further by scientists into class, order, family, genus and species. Similar appearing Cnidarians, commonly recognized by the public as a group, such as fire corals, stony corals, black corals, etc., usually fall completely within one of the lower classifications. These **Commonly Recognized Groups** are important reference keys for using this text. The predominant anatomical features that distinguish each of the eleven groups included are summarized in their corresponding Identification Group introduction. Stony corals, because of their large number, are further divided into six structural/appearance groups. All groups are also listed with a visual reference diagram under their associated group in the contents pages, in the master index on the inside front and back covers, at the top of the left page where their members are described in the text, and in bold type next to the identification photograph. It is important, as a first step in coral identification, to become familiar with these groups and their locations within the text.

# Names

Information about each species begins with the animal's common name (that used by the general public). Using common names for identification of corals by scientists is impractical because several species are known by more than one name. For example, Grooved Brain Coral, *Diploria labyrinthiformis*, is also commonly known as Depressed Brain Coral, Labyrinthine Brain Coral and just plain Brain Coral. The common names used in this text are based on previously published names. If more than one name has been published, the one most commonly used or the name which best incorporates an anatomical feature that would help the layman remember and recognize the species was selected. Previously published common names are listed in a "NOTE" at the end of the text describing each species. Several species included have never had a common name published. In these instances, a name was selected that describes a distinctive feature that can be used for visual identification. It is hoped that the common names used in this text will become standardized so future confusion will be eliminated. In this book common species names are capitalized to help set them apart, although this practice is not considered grammatically correct.

Below the common name, in italics, is the two-part scientific name. The first word (always capitalized) is the genus. The genus name is given to a group of animals with very similar physiological characteristics. The second word (never capitalized) is species. A species includes only animals that are sexually compatible and produce fertile offspring. Occasionally "sp." appears in the place of a species name, this means the species is not known. If a "n." proceeds the "sp." it means it is a new, scientifically undescribed species. Continuing below genus and species, in descending order, is a list of classification categories to which the genus and species belong. This scientific nomenclature, rooted in Latin (L.) and Greek (Gr.) is used by scientists throughout the world.

## Size

The average size range of the species divers are most likely to observe. Occasionally, the diameter of coral cups, branches, etc. is also given if this information may be useful in visual identification.

## Depth

The reported depth range in scientific literature, although species are occasionally found outside these limits. The depths at which a species is most commonly found is given in HABITAT & BEHAVIOR. Depths below the recommended safe diving limit of 130 feet are given only as a matter of scientific interest. Species that live exclusively below 130 feet are not included.

## Visual ID

Colors, markings, and anatomical differences that distinguish the species from similar appearing species. In most cases, these features are readily apparent to divers, but occasionally they are quite subtle. Generally the coral's colonial structure is described first, followed by distinguishing characteristics, and finally colors. If the colonial structure of the species is fragile, this information is also included in this section.

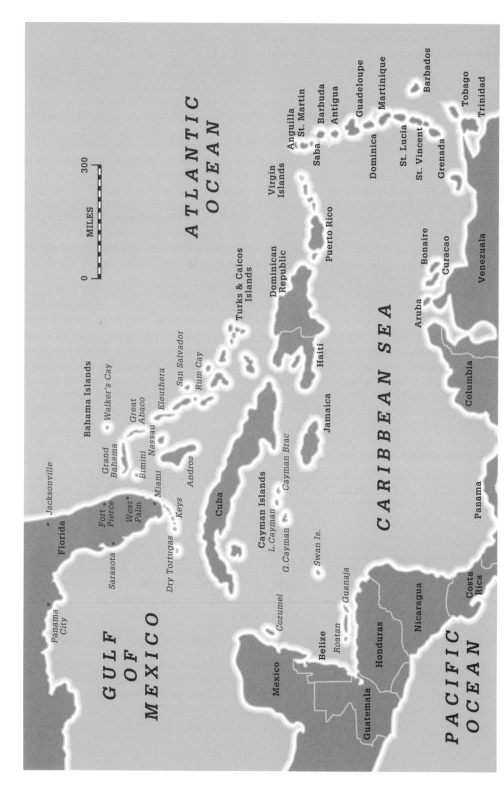

# Abundance & Distribution

*Abundance* refers to a diver's likelihood of observing a species in its normal habitat and depth range on any given dive. This is not necessarily indicative of the actual populations. Definitions are as follows:

*Abundant* - At least several sightings can be expected on nearly every dive.
*Common* - Sightings are frequent, but not necessarily on every dive.
*Occasional* - Sightings are not unusual, but not on a regular basis.
*Uncommon* - Sightings are unusual.
*Rare* - Sightings are exceptional.

*Distribution* describes where the species may be found geographically within the range of the map on the opposite page. The Turks and Caicos Islands are included as an extension of the Bahama Island chain. Described species may also be found in areas such as Bermuda and Brazil, but no attempt has been made to include this specific information in every identification, although additional data has occasionally been included. In many instances the extent of a species' geographical range is not yet known; consequently, species may occasionally be found in areas not listed. If sightings are made that do not correspond with the geographic information provided, the publisher is interested in obtaining details for updating future editions.

# Habitat & Behavior

*Habitat* is the type of underwater terrain where a particular species is likely to be found. Habitats frequented by divers, such as natural and artificial reefs, adjacent areas of sand and rubble, sea grass beds and walls are emphasized.

*Behavior* is the animal's normal activities that can be observed by a diver and used in identification.

# Effect On Divers

If a species is known to have a negative effect on divers, it is listed. The agent of the injury, how it might occur, symptoms, and recommended treatment are included where appropriate.

# Similar Species

Occasionally there are similar appearing species that are not pictured. Generally they are corals and marine plants that for one reason or another are rarely observed. Characteristics and information are given that identify and distinguish them from the species pictured.

# Note

Additional information that may help in the visual identification process such as: recent changes in classification and nomenclature, other common names also used for the same species, or details relating to the method used to identify the photographed specimen. Several photographed specimens are now part of the National Collection at the Smithsonian. Their catalog numbers (USNM) may also appear next to the specimen's photograph.

# Class Hydrozoa
(High-druh-ZO-uh/Gr. water animal)
## Hydrocorals

Hydrocorals are hydroid colonies that secrete hard, calcareous skeletons. They are often thought to be stony corals, but the resemblance is superficial. There are two types, fire and lace corals.

## FIRE CORALS

**Family Milliporidae** (Mill-LEE-pore-ih-dee/L. thousand pores)

Fire coral, or stinging coral as it is sometimes called, often produces a painful burning sensation when touched by bare skin. The pain is usually short-lived and neither severe or dangerous. For a few sensitive individuals, however, it can cause redness, welts and a rash that can last for several days. This reaction is caused by unusually powerful **batteries of stinging nematocysts** on the tentacles of the tiny polyps.

In the event of a sting, never rub the affected area or wash with fresh water or soap. Both actions can cause untriggered nematocysts to discharge. Saturating the affected area with vinegar immobilizes unspent nematocysts; a sprinkling of meat tenderizer may also help alleviate the symptoms.

The hard, calcareous skeleton of fire coral appears relatively smooth. Close observation, however, reveals a fuzzy covering which is actually the colony's tiny, hair-like polyps extending through thousands of **pinhole-sized pores**. There are two types of polyps, **sensory/stinging (dactylozooids)** and **feeding (gastrozooids)**. The feeding polyps are stout and encircled by five to nine, tall, thin sensory/stinging polyps. The polyp's gastric cavities are interconnected beneath the skeletal surface. Fire corals are generally tan to mustard with white at the tips or edges of the skeletal structure.

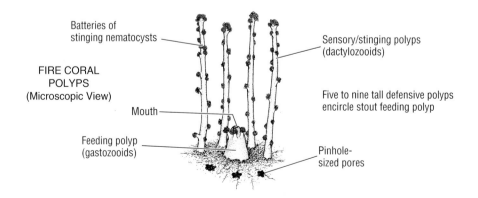

Batteries of stinging nematocysts

FIRE CORAL POLYPS
(Microscopic View)

Mouth

Feeding polyp (gastozooids)

Sensory/stinging polyps (dactylozooids)

Five to nine tall defensive polyps encircle stout feeding polyp

Pinhole-sized pores

There are three growth patterns in the Caribbean — **branching, blade** and **box**; all often encrust. Most scientists believe these represent three distinct species. Some contend, however, that each is simply a growth form of the same species.

 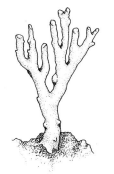 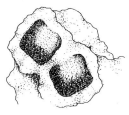

| BLADE CORAL | BRANCHING CORAL | BOX FIRE CORAL |

## LACE CORALS

**Family Stylasteridae** (Sty-LASS-ter-ih-dee/ Gr. a pillar, and a star)

The common name "lace coral" is derived from their profusely branched, hard, calcareous skeleton. Like fire corals, lace corals have both sensory/stinging polyps (dactylozooids) and feeding polyps (gastrozooids). Stout feeding polyps are encircled by five to fifteen, tall, thin sensory/stinging polyps.

The polyps extend through pores in the calcareous skeleton and form small cup-like structures, similar in appearance to those of stony corals. These tiny **cups** give outer branches a **serrated appearance**. Occasional cups are also visible on the branches thick bases. The polyp's gastric cavities are interconnected beneath the skeletal surface. Polyps have translucent hair-like appearance when extended. Small, hemispherical bumps occasionally grow on branches. Lace corals are usually shades of purple, burgundy or lavender at the base, fading to pink and white toward the branches' tips. There is only one species in the Caribbean.

Unlike fire corals, lace corals lack the powerful batteries of stinging nematocysts. They are not generally considered toxic to divers, although they can irritate sensitive skin.

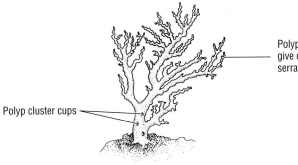

Polyps clusters cups give outer branches serrated appearance

Polyp cluster cups

LACE CORAL

**VISUAL ID:** Colonies form multiple branched structure. Branches generally cylindrical. Most commonly branch in a single plane, but occasionally in all directions. Often encrust and overgrow gorgonian colonies, taking on their shape. Surface texture smooth with numerous pin-hole size pores. When the tiny polyps protrude, they appear as short, fine hair. Tan to mustard and brown; branch tips white.

**ABUNDANCE & DISTRIBUTION:** Abundant to common Florida, Bahamas, Caribbean.

**HABITAT & BEHAVIOR:** Inhabit all marine environments. The only one of the three fire corals that commonly grows deeper than 30 feet and is relatively uncommon in shallow surge zones.

**EFFECT ON DIVERS:** Toxic; contact with bare skin will produce an intense, but usually short-lived, sting. May cause minor redness, welts and rash.

**Encrusting Substrate**

**Encrusting Sea Feather Plume**

*Millepora alcicornis*
FAMILY:
**Fire Corals**
Milleporidae

SIZE: 1-18 in.
DEPTH: 3-130 ft.

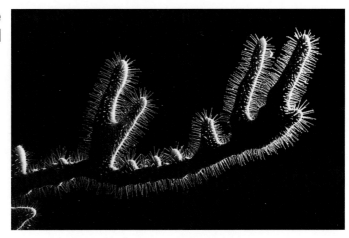

**Hair-Like
Polyp Detail**

**Encrusting
Common Sea Fan**

17

**VISUAL ID:** Colonies form thin, upright blades or plates that extend from an encrusting base. Outer edge of blades uneven with multiple extensions or short branches. Surface texture smooth with numerous pin-hole size pores. When the tiny polyps protrude, they appear as short, fine hair. Tan to mustard and brown; blade edges white.

**ABUNDANCE & DISTRIBUTION:** Abundant to common Florida, Bahamas, Caribbean.

**HABITAT & BEHAVIOR:** Inhabit shallow water reef tops. Usually in areas with some water movement; most common in areas with constant surge.

**EFFECT ON DIVERS:** Toxic; contact with bare skin will produce an intense, but usually short-lived, sting. May cause minor redness, welts and rash.

**Reef Top Colony**

**VISUAL ID:** Colonies form open-ended, thick-walled, box-like structures that extend upward from an encrusting base. Often join to form honeycomb pattern or encrust in rippled wave-like pattern. Surface texture smooth with numerous pin-hole size pores. When the tiny polyps protrude, they appear as short, fine hair. Tan to mustard brown, with reddish to pink or lavender tints that are distinctive of this species; open end edges of boxes whitish.

**ABUNDANCE & DISTRIBUTION:** Common to occasional Dominican Republic southward through Lesser Antilles to Brazil. Not reported Florida, Bahamas, North or West Caribbean.

**HABITAT & BEHAVIOR:** Inhabit shallow water reef tops. Usually in areas with some water movement, most common in areas with regular surge.

**EFFECT ON DIVERS:** Not considered toxic; although may sting sensitive skin.

### BLADE FIRE CORAL
*Millepora complanata*
FAMILY:
**Fire Corals**
Milleporidae

SIZE: 1-18 in.
DEPTH: 0-45 ft

**Hair-Like
Polyp Detail**

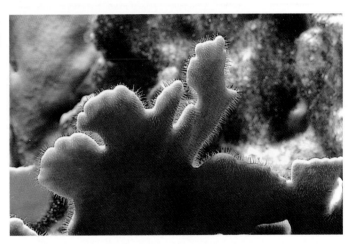

### BOX FIRE CORAL
*Millepora squarrosa*
FAMILY:
**Fire Corals**
Milleporidae

SIZE: ¹/₂-2 in.
DEPTH: 6-30 ft.

*continued next page*

**VISUAL ID:** Colonies form fan-like structures of branches. The cylindrical branches taper from base to tip. Tiny cups, formed by the feeding and the encircling stinging polyps, give outer branches a serrated appearance. Occasional cups also visible on branches' thick base. Polyps have translucent hair-like appearance when extended. Small, hemispherical bumps occasionally grow on branches. Purple to burgundy or lavender near colony base, fading to pink and white toward branch tips. Occasionally all white.

**ABUNDANCE & DISTRIBUTION:** Common South Florida, Bahamas, Caribbean.

**HABITAT & BEHAVIOR:** Inhabit protected, shaded areas of reefs. Often in cracks, under ledge overhangs, caves and recesses.

**EFFECT ON DIVERS:** Not considered toxic, although may sting sensitive bare skin.

## BOX FIRE CORAL
*continued from
previous page*
### Growth Patterns

## ROSE LACE CORAL
*Stylaster roseus*
FAMILY:
**Lace Corals**
Stylasteridae

SIZE: 1-4 in.
DEPTH: 15-100 ft.

### Color Varieties

# CLASS ANTHOZOA
(An-thuh-ZO-uh/L. flower-like animal)

# SUBCLASS OCTOCORALLIA
(Octo-core-AL-ee-uh/Gr. & L. eight and coral animal)

## Gorgonians, Telestaceans, Soft Corals

**Octocorallian polyps** have **eight tentacles** that bear tiny pinnate (feather-like) projections called **pinnules**. Octocoral colors come from one or a combination of three sources: pigments in the polyps' tissues; intracellular symbiotic algae in the polyps' tissues, called zooxanthellae (zo-zan-THEL-ee); and/or coloring minerals in the calcareous spicules of the colonial structure. Colors often vary between colonies of the same species and are rarely useful in the identification process. For those few species where color is a reliable identification characteristic, a dive light is necessary to reveal the true shade underwater. Occasionally, members of this subclass are inaccurately referred to as "horny corals" because their supporting skeletal material superficially resembles the horn-like protein of turtle shells, and the hoofs, horns, and antlers of mammals.

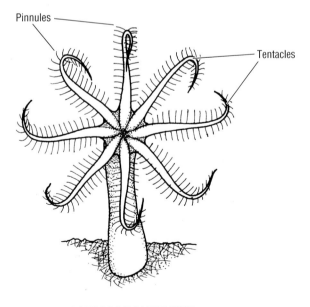

Pinnules

Tentacles

OCTOCORALLIAN POLYP

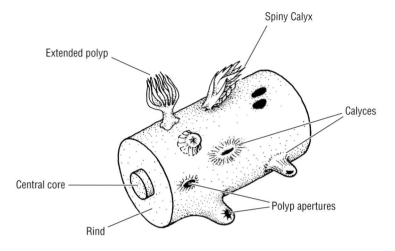

Spiny Calyx

Extended polyp

Calyces

Central core

Polyp apertures

Rind

GORGONIAN BRANCH
(Showing calyx and aperture variations)

# GORGONIANS

Traditionally **Order Gorgonacea** (Gore-GON-ace-ee-ah/
Gr. ugly, terrible or myth of three sisters with snakes for hair)
**Suborders Scleraxonia** and **Holaxonia**

Gorgonians is the preferred name for this large group of octocorallians; however, they are commonly called "soft corals" because of the colonies' lack of a hard, rigid, permanent skeletons. The common name soft coral should be used when referring to members of the Family Nephtheidae, abundant in the Indo-Pacific. Gorgonians include the animal colonies known as sea rods, flat sea whips, sea feather plumes, sea fans and orange sea whips. To assist in visual identification, species have been arranged by the colony's shape and common name, rather than their traditional scientific grouping. In most instances this method keeps members of the same family and genus together.

The stems and branches of all gorgonians have a central skeleton or axis. The **central core** in the Suborder Scleraxonia is composed of either tightly bound or fused calcareous spicules. A wood-like core typifies the Suborder Holaxonia. The core is surrounded by gelatinous material called the **rind**. **Polyps** are embedded in the rind and extend their tentacles and bodies from surface openings (apertures). The arrangement of the polyps (in rows, alternating bands, randomly scattered, etc.) is often helpful in the identification process. The shape of **polyp apertures** and the rims around them, called **calyces (calyx, singular)**, are often used to determine the genus and, occasionally, species.

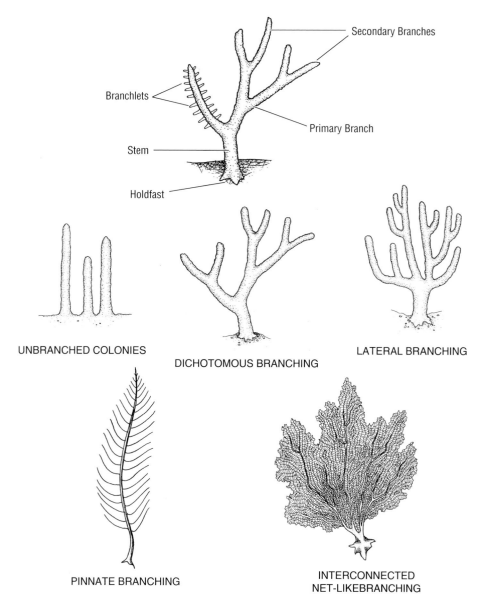

Secondary Branches

Branchlets

Primary Branch

Stem

Holdfast

UNBRANCHED COLONIES

DICHOTOMOUS BRANCHING

LATERAL BRANCHING

PINNATE BRANCHING

INTERCONNECTED
NET-LIKEBRANCHING

Most gorgonian colonies are attached to the substrate by a single **holdfast** at the base of a **stem** that usually **branches**. This branching pattern, which includes **unbranched, dichotomous, lateral and pinnate branching** and **interconnected net-like branching,** is often characteristic of the genus and is occasionally distinctive in determining a species. Branching may be in a single plane or bushy. **Branchlets** are small, usually profuse, branches that in some species line the sides of the primary branches.

Unfortunately, less than half of the 60-70 reef gorgonians can be visually identified to species underwater. Positive identification requires microscopic examination of the location, pattern, shape and size of the skeletal spicules embedded in the polyp's and colony's common tissue.

24

# TELESTACEANS

### Order Alcyonanea – Suborder Stolonifera
### Family Clavulariidae – Subfamily Telestinae
Traditionally **Order Telestacea** (Tell-uh-STAY-see-ah/ Gr. poet)

Telestacean colonies grow by extending a long **terminal polyp** that produces a stem with short side branches tipped with **daughter polyps**. The polyps are brilliant white. They can often be identified by stem color, depth and geographical location. The stem's color, however, is frequently obscured by encrusting algae, sponge, and other organisms. Telestaceans are generally found in areas of moderate turbidity, and only rarely occur on clear water reefs. They are considered a fouling organism.

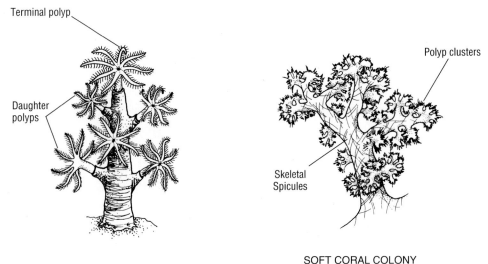

Terminal polyp

Daughter polyps

Polyp clusters

Skeletal Spicules

TELESTACEAN COLONY

SOFT CORAL COLONY

# SOFT CORALS

### Order Alcyonacea (Al-see-NAY-see-ah/Gr. a kingfisher)
### Family Nephtheidae (NEF-the-ih-dee/ Gr. lady of the house)

Soft corals resemble thick-trunked, branched trees. **Polyps** are clumped on the branch tips, and occasionally in small clusters and/or solitary polyps on the trunk or branches' surface. The pliable colony is composed of a rubbery or thick jelly-like material that is often translucent with the embedded **skeletal spicules** clearly visible. Colors are a wide range of pastel shades. Although profuse on Indo-Pacific reefs, there are only a few species in the tropical Western Atlantic and these usually occur far below safe diving limits. On occasion, however, a few colonies may grow as shallow as 100 feet.

# Gorgonians

**VISUAL ID:** Colonies form one to several erect, unbranched, cylindrical rods, arising from a common encrusting base. When extended, large polyps give colony "hairy" appearance. Area around pore-like polyp apertures often swollen. Rods (rind) violet to purple and purple-gray, occasionally with some tints of brown or tan; polyps greenish brown to brown and brownish gray. Colonies also form thick encrustations without any erect rod structures. Occasionally encrust branches of other gorgonians. (Compare similar appearing Encrusting Gorgonian [next] distinguished by tan rind and polyps.)

**ABUNDANCE & DISTRIBUTION:** Abundant to common South Florida, Bahamas, Caribbean.

**HABITAT & BEHAVIOR:** Inhabit most reef environments, especially shallow fringing, patch and back reef areas.

**NOTE:** Also commonly known as "Deadman's Fingers."

**Comparison of Colonies with Polyps Extended and Retracted: Note Purplish Shades of Rind**

## CORKY SEA FINGER
*Briareum asbestinum*
SUBORDER:
Scleraxonia
FAMILY:
Briareidae

SIZE: Colony height
$^1/_2$ - 24 in.
DEPTH: 3 - 100 ft.

## Colony Encrusting
## Sea Feather Plume

## Comparison of Polyps
## Extended and Retracted

## Encrusting Variety,
## Polyp Detail
[far left]
## Encrusting Large Area
[near left]

27

# Gorgonians

**VISUAL ID:** Colonies form, encrusting mats. Extended polyps and tentacles appear as fine hair. When polyps retracted, rind appears smooth and leather-like, and apertures appear as pin-sized pores, rarely with slightly projecting calyces. Tan, underside reddish, apertures often whitish. (Similar encrusting variety of Corky Sea Fingers [previous] distinguished by thick, purplish rind and larger, darker polyps, often area around polyp apertures swollen.)

**ABUNDANCE & DISTRIBUTION:** Occasional Florida, Bahamas, Caribbean.

**HABITAT & BEHAVIOR:** Inhabit most reef environments, especially shallow fringing, patch and back reef areas.

**Note Fine, "Hair-like" Appearance of Extended Polyps**

**VISUAL ID:** Colonies are quite bushy, but grow in flat, vertical planes. Tend to branch laterally, with only occasional dichotomous branching. (Similar Bent Sea Rod [next] tends to branch dichotomously.) The contrast of light yellow-brown to brown polyps against dark brown to black stalks (rind) is a distinctive characteristic of this species. When polyps retracted, area around apertures is flat or protrudes only slightly.

**ABUNDANCE & DISTRIBUTION:** Common South Florida, Bahamas, Caribbean.

**HABITAT & BEHAVIOR:** Inhabit clear water patch reefs. Colonies growing in deeper water tend to have more slender branches in denser concentrations and grow taller than their shallow water counterparts.

### ENCRUSTING GORGONIAN
*Erythropodium caribaeorum*
SUBORDER:
Scleraxonia
FAMILY:
Anthothelidae

SIZE: 3 in. - 3 ft.
DEPTH: 3 - 100 ft.

**Comparison of Extended and Retracted Polyps: Note Smooth Texture of Rind**

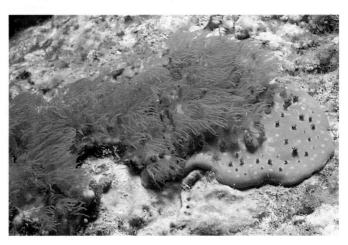

### BLACK SEA ROD
*Plexaura homomalla*
SUBORDER:
Holaxonia
FAMILY:
Plexauridae

SIZE: Colony height
½ - 2 ft.
DEPTH: 4 - 200 ft.

*continued next page*

# Gorgonians

**Branch Detail,
Polyps Retracted**

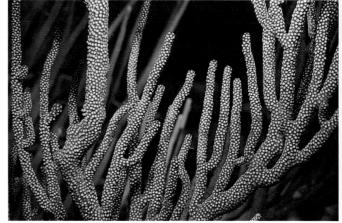

**VISUAL ID:** Colonies usually grow in flat, vertical planes with profuse dichotomous branching. (Similar Black Sea Rod [previous] tend to branch laterally.) Occasionally bushy, branching in all directions. Pale to tan, yellow-brown, brown, reddish purple and purple. Polyps occasionally lighter than stalk. When polyps retracted, rim of aperture is only slightly raised with a small lip or shelf around the inside.

**ABUNDANCE & DISTRIBUTION:** Common South Florida, Bahamas, Caribbean.

**HABITAT & BEHAVIOR:** Inhabit clear water patch reefs.

**Branch Detail,
Polyps Retracted**

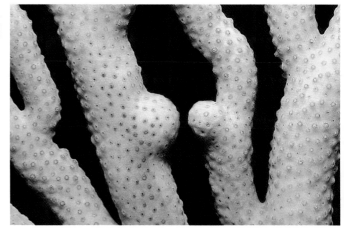

### BLACK SEA ROD

*continued from
previous page*

**Small Colony
Branch Detail,
Polyps Extended**

### BENT SEA ROD

*Plexaura flexuosa*

SUBORDER:
Holaxonia
FAMILY:
Plexauridae

SIZE: Colony height
6 - 16 in.
DEPTH: 4 - 150 ft.

**Branching in
All Directions**

# Gorgonians

**VISUAL ID:** Sea rod colonies of this genus can be recognized when their polyps are retracted, leaving apertures that appear as round to oval pores without raised rims (calyces). All four species of this genus are so individually variable in appearance, and yet similar to one another, that they cannot easily be distinguished visually. Microscopic examination is required for positive identification. Colonies are generally bushy with stout stalks and branch dichotomously. Colors vary greatly from light brown to yellow-brown, brown, reddish purple, purple and gray.

**ABUNDANCE & DISTRIBUTION:** Common South Florida, Bahamas, Caribbean.

**HABITAT & BEHAVIOR:** Inhabit most clear water reef environments.

**Note Pore-like Polyp Aperture without Raised Calyces**

**POROUS SEA RODS**
*Pseudoplexaura sp.*
SUBORDER:
Holaxonia
FAMILY:
Plexauridae

SIZE: Colony height
¹/₂ - 7 ft.
DEPTH: 3 - 250 ft.

**Note Pore-like
Polyp Apertures**

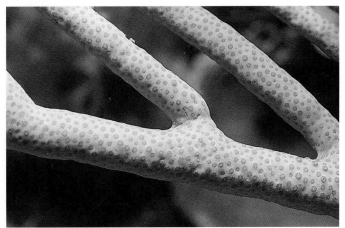

**Tall Colony**
[far left]

**Branch Detail**
[near left]

**Bush-like Colony**

**VISUAL ID:** Sea rod colonies of this genus can be recognized when their polyps are retracted, leaving prominently extended calyces (with one exception, *E. knighti*, whose polyp apertures resemble those of Porous Sea Rods). Most branch laterally in a flat plane that resembles a candelabrum. Only a few of the over one dozen species can be distinguished underwater. All remaining species of this genus are so individually variable in appearance, and yet similar to one another, that they cannot easily be distinguished visually. Microscopic examination is required for positive identification. Colors vary greatly from light brown through yellow-brown, brown, reddish purple, purple and gray.

**ABUNDANCE & DISTRIBUTION:** Common South Florida, Bahamas, Caribbean.

**HABITAT & BEHAVIOR:** Inhabit most reef environments and adjacent sandy substrates.

**Polyp Detail**

**VISUAL ID:** The close-set, swollen, tubular calyces of these candelabrum-shaped colonies easily distinguish them from other members of the genus. Colonies compact with stout branches. Light yellowish brown.

**ABUNDANCE & DISTRIBUTION:** Common Northwest Caribbean; uncommon to occasional South Florida, Bahamas, eastern and southern Caribbean.

**HABITAT & BEHAVIOR:** Inhabit most reef environments, from shallow, turbulent hard bottoms to patch reefs, deeper outer reefs and along wall lips.

**SIMILAR SPECIES:** Tube-knob Candelabrum, *E. laxispica*, distinguished by longer, more widely spaced, tube-like calyces. Uncommon to rare.

## KNOBBY SEA RODS
*Eunicea sp.*
**SUBORDER:**
Holaxonia
**FAMILY:**
Plexauridae

**SIZE:** Colony height
$^1/_2$ - 3 ft.
**DEPTH:** 3 - 100 ft.

### Knobby Calyx Detail

## SWOLLEN-KNOB CANDELABRUM
*Eunicea mammosa*
**SUBORDER:**
Holaxonia
**FAMILY:**
Plexauridae

**SIZE:** Colony height
$^3/_4$ - 1 ft.
**DEPTH:** 5 - 90 ft.

*continued next page*

**35**

**Calyx Detail:
Note Close-set,
Swollen Tubular Form**

**VISUAL ID:** The diagonally upward projecting calyces distinguish this species from other members of the genus. In side view the calyces appear as tiny shelves with diagonal supports. Calyces' lower lips slightly upturned. Colonies grow in two forms: forma *succinea* are low, wide, candelabrum-shaped with thick end branches; forma *plantaginea* are tall and bushy with thin end branches, calyces' lower lips more upturned. (Similar Warty Sea Rod [next] distinguished by thicker branches and gaping calyces.) Light yellowish brown to brown.

**ABUNDANCE & DISTRIBUTION:** Common South Florida, Bahamas, Caribbean.

**HABITAT & BEHAVIOR:** Inhabit shallow, turbulent hard bottoms and patch reefs.

**Calyx Detail:
Note Shelf-like
Appearance**

## SWOLLEN-KNOB CANDELABRUM
*continued from previous page*

**Colony with Polyps Retracted**

---

## SHELF-KNOB SEA ROD
*Eunicea succinea*

SUBORDER:
Holaxonia
FAMILY:
Plexauridae

**forma *succinea***

SIZE: Colony height
³/₄ - 2 ft.
DEPTH: 5 - 50 ft.

**forma *plantaginea***

**VISUAL ID:** Only Knobby Sea Rod colony with thick, cylindrical, non-tapering branches that is tall, bushy, and does not branch in a single plane. (Can be confused with Shelf-knob Sea Rod, forma *plantaginea* [previous], distinguished by their thinner end branches and shelf-like calyces.) Dichotomous branching. Extended polyps give colony yellowish brown appearance. Calyces low and gaping.

**ABUNDANCE & DISTRIBUTION:** Common South Florida, Bahamas, Caribbean.

**HABITAT & BEHAVIOR:** Inhabit most reef environments; most common on inshore reefs.

**Polyp Detail**

**VISUAL ID:** When fully contracted the low, circular, somewhat swollen calyces with round, central apertures distinguish this species from other members of the genus. Often form low, bushy, shrub-like colonies, occasionally tall with widely spaced branches. Rods light to dark gray; polyps yellow-brown to brown.

**ABUNDANCE & DISTRIBUTION:** Common to occasional South Florida, Bahamas, Caribbean.

**HABITAT & BEHAVIOR:** Inhabit shallow, turbulent hard bottoms and patch reefs.

### WARTY SEA ROD

*Eunicea calyculata*

**SUBORDER:**
Holaxonia
**FAMILY:**
Plexauridae

**SIZE:** Colony height
1 - 3 ft.
**DEPTH:** 10 - 110 ft.

### Calyx Detail

### DOUGHNUT SEA ROD

*Eunicea fusca*

**SUBORDER:**
Holaxonia
**FAMILY:**
Plexauridae

**SIZE:** Colony height
$^1/_2$ - $1^1/_2$ ft.
**DEPTH:** 10 - 75 ft.

*continued next page*

**VISUAL ID:** Sea rod colonies of this genus can be recognized when their polyps are retracted, leaving elliptical or slit-like apertures that may or may not have slightly raised rims (calyces). With one exception, Giant Slit-pore Sea Rod (next), all of the six species of this genus are so individually variable in appearance, and yet similar to one another, that they cannot easily be distinguished visually. Microscopic examination is required for positive identification. Colonies are generally bushy with stout stalks, and branch dichotomously. Colors vary greatly from light brown to yellow-brown, brown, reddish purple, purple and gray.

**ABUNDANCE & DISTRIBUTION:** Common South Florida, Bahamas, Caribbean.

**HABITAT & BEHAVIOR:** Inhabit most clear water reef environments.

**Colony with Polyps Retracted**

## DOUGHNUT SEA ROD
*continued from*
*previous page*

**Comparison
of Doughnut
Sea Rod, (left) and
Bent Sea Rod (right)**

**Polyp Detail**
[far left]

**Calyx Detail**
[near left]

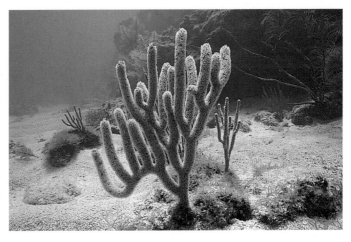

## SLIT-PORE SEA RODS
*Plexaurella sp.*
SUBORDER:
Holaxonia
FAMILY:
Plexauridae

SIZE: Colony height
$^{1}/_{2}$ - 3 $^{1}/_{2}$ ft.
DEPTH: 3 - 160 ft.

**Retracted Polyp Detail:
Note Slit-like Aperture**

**VISUAL ID:** Colonies very tall with thick stalks and sparse, dichotomous branching. Branch tips usually somewhat enlarged. Slit-like apertures of retracted polyps are on slightly raised, well-separated mounds. Pale gray to tan or light brown.

**ABUNDANCE & DISTRIBUTION:** Common to occasional South Florida, Bahamas, Caribbean.

**HABITAT & BEHAVIOR:** Primarily inhabit clear water patch and fore reefs.

**NOTE:** Also commonly known as "Nodding Plexaurella."

**Retracted Polyp Detail:
Note Slightly Raised Lips
and Slit-like Pores**

**VISUAL ID:** Low, broad fan-shaped colonies, branched laterally with only occasional dichotomous secondary branching, all in single planes. Branches tend to be tightly compacted. Hard, rough calyces with sharply spiked tips extend prominently. Pale yellowish brown to light brown; polyps white.

**ABUNDANCE & DISTRIBUTION:** Common to occasional South Florida, Bahamas, Caribbean.

**HABITAT & BEHAVIOR:** Inhabit wide range of shallow to moderate environments.

**NOTE:** Photographed specimen was collected and visual identification confirmed by examination of wood-like central branch axis which is conspicuously flattened in this species.

**SIMILAR SPECIES:** Open Spiny Sea Fan, *M. atlantica*, visually distinguished by their tendency to be taller and having more open branching. Uncommon. Positive identification requires specimen examination of the wood-like central branch axis which is not conspicuously flattened.

## GIANT SLIT-PORE SEA ROD

*Plexaurella nutans*

SUBORDER:
Holaxonia
FAMILY:
Plexauridae

SIZE: Colony height
2 - 4 ½ ft.
DEPTH: 30 - 160 ft.

## SPINY SEA FAN

*Muricea muricata*

SUBORDER:
Holaxonia
FAMILY:
Plexauridae

SIZE: Colony height
4 - 12 in.
DEPTH: 0 - 60 ft.

*continued next page*

**VISUAL ID:** Colonies have open pinnate branching in single planes; older colonies may be somewhat bushy. Branchlets short, stiff and widely spaced. Hard, rough calyces; each has a distinctive, long, sharp terminal spine. Branches whitish to light gray or yellow-brown; polyps yellowish brown.

**ABUNDANCE & DISTRIBUTION:** Occasional Caribbean.

**HABITAT & BEHAVIOR:** Inhabit clear water, moderate to deep fore reef environments.

**SIMILAR SPECIES:** Pinnate Spiney Sea Fan, *M. pendula*, because of its distinctive red color is described on page 77.

**Branch/Polyp Detail:
Note Open Pinnate
Branching**

**SPINY SEA FAN**
*continued from
previous page*
**Unusually Tall Colony**

**Polyp Detail**
[far left]
**Calyx Detail**
[near left]

**LONG SPINE SEA FAN**
*Muricea pinnata*
SUBORDER:
Holaxonia
FAMILY:
Plexauridae

SIZE: Colony height
8 - 18 in.
DEPTH: 40 - 120 ft.

**Branch/Calyx Detail:
Note Long, Terminal
Spines**

45

# Gorgonians

**VISUAL ID:** Tall, bushy colonies, not branched in single planes. Branched laterally near base, but toward top tend to branch pinnately. Hard, rough, close-set calyces extend prominently with sharply spiked lower lips. Branches yellow to yellowish brown, orange or amber; polyps white. (Similar Delicate Spiny Sea Rod [next] can usually be distinguished by their bluish white to gray branches, thinner branches, more projecting calyx lips and deeper habitat.)

**ABUNDANCE & DISTRIBUTION:** Common to occasional Florida's west coast and from West Palm through the Keys, Bahamas, Caribbean.

**HABITAT & BEHAVIOR:** Inhabit wide range of shallow to moderate environments, from sandy bottoms to sloping rocky substrates and patch reefs.

**NOTE:** Small sample of pictured specimen was collected and visual identification confirmed by microscopic examination of spicules.

**Polyp Detail**

**VISUAL ID:** Tall, bushy colonies, laterally branched, but not in single planes. Branches slender, flexible and long. Narrow, hard, rough calyces extend prominently upward with sharply spiked lower lips. Branches bluish gray to bluish white, occasionally yellowish; polyps white. (Compare similar Orange Spiny Sea Rod [previous].)

**ABUNDANCE & DISTRIBUTION:** Common to occasional Florida's west coast and from West Palm through the Keys, Bahamas, Caribbean.

**HABITAT & BEHAVIOR:** Inhabit wide range of moderate to deep environments, from sloping rocky substrates to patch reefs.

**NOTE:** Small sample of pictured specimen was collected and visual identification confirmed by microscopic examination of spicules.

**ORANGE SPINY
SEA ROD**

*Muricea elongata*

SUBORDER:
Holaxonia
FAMILY:
Plexauridae

SIZE: Colony height
1 - 1½ ft.
DEPTH: 10 - 70 ft.

**Branch/Calyx Detail:
Note Orangish Color**

**DELICATE SPINY
SEA ROD**

*Muricea laxa*

SUBORDER:
Holaxonia
FAMILY:
Plexauridae

SIZE: Colony height
8 - 12 in.
DEPTH: 60 - 420 ft.

*continued next page*

**Branch/Polyp Detail**

**VISUAL ID:** Colonies form bushy clusters of tall, plume-like branches. Numerous short, slender, round branchlets extend from all sides of main branches. Small, closely set polyp apertures are scattered randomly on all sides of main and secondary branches. (Similar Sea Feather Plumes [next] have polyps in rows, series or bands.) Apertures have small, lower shelf-like lips, giving the surface a somewhat rough texture. Most commonly purple, occasionally gray, and may be tinged with yellow.

**ABUNDANCE & DISTRIBUTION:** Common South Florida, Bahamas, Caribbean.

**HABITAT & BEHAVIOR:** Inhabit most clear water patch reef environments.

**ADDITIONAL SPECIES:** Sulphur Sea Plume, *M. sulphurea*, yellow, low, bushy, shrub-like colonies; secondary branches on all sides of main branches and polyps randomly scattered on all sides; Puerto Rico through Lesser Antilles. Deep Water Sea Plume, *M. petila*, tall, main branches with widely spaced, pinnately branching secondary branches; violet to lavender; below 100 feet; South Florida, Bahamas.

**Branch Detail:
Note Branchlets
Extend in All Directions**

**DELICATE SPINY SEA ROD**
*continued from previous page*

**Branch/Calyx Detail: Note Bluish Gray Color**

**ROUGH SEA PLUME**
*Muriceopsis flavida*
SUBORDER:
Holaxonia
FAMILY:
Plexauridae

SIZE: Colony height
8 - 30 in.
DEPTH: 3 - 110 ft.

**Gray Variety**

# Gorgonians

**VISUAL ID:** Bushy clusters of tall, feather-like plumes typify this genus. Pinnately branching secondary branches or branchlets, lying more or less in single planes, extend from the main branches. Polyps in rows, series or bands, rather than random distribution on all sides of branch. Calyces absent or indistinct. Most commonly purple to gray branches, occasionally bright to pale yellow or yellow-brown. Polyps generally cream to brownish or grayish. With two exceptions, Slimy Sea Plume [next] and Bipinnate Sea Plume [following], all of the remaining dozen or so species of this genus are so individually variable in appearance, and yet similar to one another, that they cannot easily be distinguished visually. Microscopic examination is required for positive identification.

**ABUNDANCE & DISTRIBUTION:** Common South Florida, Bahamas, Caribbean.

**HABITAT & BEHAVIOR:** Inhabit most reef environments, from shallow, seaward sandy areas to patch reefs to deep clear water reefs along drop-offs.

**Several Species Can Exceed Seven Feet in Height**

**VISUAL ID:** Colonies form bushy clusters of tall, feather-like plumes. Long branchlets extend pinnately from primary branches. Primary branches most commonly purple to violet, occasionally pale yellow. Living colonies produce large amounts of mucus, causing the branches to feel slimy, distinguishing them from similar appearing species. (To avoid injury to a colony it should only be lightly touched near the base, which will feel soft, slick and slimy.)

**ABUNDANCE & DISTRIBUTION:** Common South Florida, Bahamas, Caribbean.

**HABITAT & BEHAVIOR:** Inhabit most reef environments, from shallow hard bottoms to patch reefs to deep clear water reefs along drop-offs.

### SEA PLUMES
*Pseudopterogorgia sp.*
SUBORDER:
Holaxonia
FAMILY:
Gorgoniidae

SIZE: Colony height
1 - 7 ft.
DEPTH: 3 - 180 ft.

### Large Colony with Polyps Retracted

### SLIMY SEA PLUME
*Pseudopterogorgia
americana*
SUBORDER:
Holaxonia
FAMILY:
Gorgoniidae

SIZE: Colony height
2 $\frac{1}{2}$ - 3 $\frac{1}{2}$ ft.
DEPTH: 5 - 150 ft.

# Gorgonians

**VISUAL ID:** Colonies generally grow in single planes with broadly spread primary and secondary branches. Paired branchlets extend from branches at regularly spaced intervals. These branchlets, distinctive of this species, are short, blunt, stiff and extend directly opposite one another at almost right angles. Branches most commonly purple to violet, occasionally bright yellow to whitish.

**ABUNDANCE & DISTRIBUTION:** Common South Florida, Bahamas, Caribbean.

**HABITAT & BEHAVIOR:** Inhabit moderate to deep, clear water patch reefs.

**VISUAL ID:** Small, bushy and highly branched colonies. Branches quite flat and narrow with polyps extending from swollen, slit-like apertures along the thin edges. (Similar Grooved-blade Sea Whip [next] is distinguished by polyps extending from common groove along thin edges.) Branches bright yellow to green to olive with purple edges, occasionally all purple; polyps white to cream.

**ABUNDANCE & DISTRIBUTION:** Common South Florida, Bahamas, Caribbean. Can be abundant in localized areas.

**HABITAT & BEHAVIOR:** Inhabit a wide range of shallower, inshore environments, from back reef areas to patch reefs.

## BIPINNATE SEA PLUME
*Pseudopterogorgia bipinnata*
SUBORDER:
Holaxonia
FAMILY:
Gorgoniidae

SIZE: Colony height
1 - 2 ft.
DEPTH: 45 - 180 ft.

**Colony with Polyps Retracted**

**Branch Detail: Polyps Extended**
[far left]

**Branch Detail: Polyps Retracted**
[near left]

## YELLOW SEA WHIP
*Pterogorgia citrina*
SUBORDER:
Holaxonia
FAMILY:
Gorgoniidae

SIZE: Colony height
4 - 12 in.
Branch width ¼ in.
DEPTH: 3 - 40 ft.

*continued next page*

**53**

# Gorgonians

**VISUAL ID:** Colonies heavily branched, more or less in single planes. Long, flexible branches quite flat and wide, tapering somewhat from base to end. Polyps extend from a groove that runs along the thin edges. (Similar Yellow Sea Whip [previous] is distinguished by polyps extending from slit-like apertures along thin edges.) Branches olive to gray, occasionally light purple; polyps white to cream.

**ABUNDANCE & DISTRIBUTION:** Occasional South Florida, Bahamas, Caribbean.

**HABITAT & BEHAVIOR:** Inhabit a wide range of inshore environments, from back reef areas of sand and rubble to patch reefs of moderate depth.

**Polyp/Groove Detail**

**YELLOW SEA WHIP**
*continued from
previous page*
**Color Variety**

**Calyx/Polyp Detail:
Note Polyps do not
Extend From
a Slit-like Groove**
[far left]
**Color Variety**
[near left]

**GROOVED-BLADE
SEA WHIP**
*Pterogorgia
guadalupensis*
SUBORDER:
Holaxonia
FAMILY:
Gorgoniidae

SIZE: Colony height
$^{1}/_{2}$ - 2 ft.
Branch width $^{1}/_{4}$ - $^{1}/_{2}$ in.
DEPTH: 3 - 60 ft.

**Purplish Variety**

**VISUAL ID:** Colonies large, bushy and highly branched. A cross-section of a branch is "Y" or "X" shaped. Branches taper from bases toward the terminal ends and often twist. Ends may occasionally be a flattened blade-shape. Polyps extend from a groove that runs along the branches' thin edges. Olive to brown to gray, occasionally purple or with purplish tints. Edge of grooves usually purple; polyps white to cream.

**ABUNDANCE & DISTRIBUTION:** Common to occasional South Florida, Bahamas, Caribbean. Can be abundant in localized areas.

**HABITAT & BEHAVIOR:** Inhabit a wide range of inshore environments, from back reef areas of sand and rubble to patch reefs of moderate depth.

**Polyp/Groove Detail**

**VISUAL ID:** Colonies form large fans that grow in single planes. Fans are composed of tightly-meshed, interconnected network of branches that are round or slightly flattened on the outer surface. (Compare similar Venus Sea Fan [next].) In Florida always purple, remainder of range commonly purple, occasionally yellow or brownish.

**ABUNDANCE & DISTRIBUTION:** Common South Florida, Bahamas, Caribbean.

**HABITAT & BEHAVIOR:** Prefer clear water with some movement. Inhabit the seaward side of shallow reefs, slopes and patch reefs. Only occasionally on reefs and along the lips of drop-offs deeper than 50 feet.

## ANGULAR SEA WHIP
*Pterogorgia anceps*
SUBORDER:
Holaxonia
FAMILY:
Gorgoniidae

**SIZE:** Colony height
1 - 2 ft.
Branch width $^1/_8$ - $^1/_4$ in.
**DEPTH:** 12 - 65 ft.

### Colony with Polyps Retracted

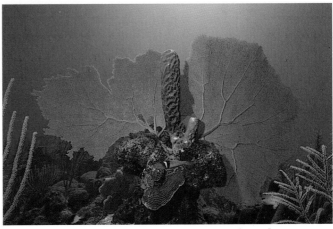

## COMMON SEA FAN
*Gorgonia ventalina*
SUBORDER:
Holaxonia
FAMILY:
Gorgoniidae

**SIZE:** Colony height
2 - 6 ft.
**DEPTH:** 3 - 100 ft.

*continued next page*

**57**

**Branch Detail: Outer Surface Flattened**
[far left]

**VISUAL ID:** Colonies form large fans that grow in single planes. Fans are composed of tightly-meshed, interconnected network of branches. Branches' inner edges are distinctly flattened at right angles to the fans' surfaces. (Compare similar Common Sea Fan [previous].) Occasionally have small branchlets growing from their flat sides. Commonly yellow, occasionally lavender to gray.

**ABUNDANCE & DISTRIBUTION:** Abundant Bahamas; common to uncommon Caribbean; rare South Florida.

**HABITAT & BEHAVIOR:** Prefer clear water with some movement. Commonly inhabit the seaward side of shallow reef slopes and patch reefs. Only occasionally on reefs and along lips of drop-offs deeper than 35 feet. In Caribbean often inhabit shallow back reef areas.

**NOTE:** Also commonly known as "Bahamian Sea Fan."

**Branching Detail: Note Flattening at Right Angle to Fan's Surface**

**COMMON SEA FAN**
*continued from
previous page*

**VENUS SEA FAN**
*Gorgonia flabellum*
SUBORDER:
Holaxonia
FAMILY:
Gorgoniidae

SIZE: Colony height
2 - 3 ½ ft.
DEPTH: 3 - 100 ft.

**Color Varieties**

**VISUAL ID:** Colonies form small fans that grow in single planes. Fans are composed of a widely-meshed pattern of branches. Secondary branches extending from ascending primary branches are generally pinnate and do not always unite or interconnect. In deep water white to pale violet or yellow; in shallow water tend to be yellow, occasionally with purplish tints.

**ABUNDANCE & DISTRIBUTION:** Occasional Caribbean. Not known from Florida or Bahamas.

**HABITAT & BEHAVIOR:** Prefer clear water with some movement. Inhabit wide range of reef environments, but most abundant below 50 feet where Common and Venus Sea Fans [previous] are not as numerous.

**Branch Structure Detail:
Note Sparse
Interconnecting of
Branches**

**VISUAL ID:** Branch dichotomously in single planes to form huge fan-shaped colonies. Outer surfaces of branches flattened with polyps extending in two parallel rows from narrow inner edges. Red-brown to orange-brown, dark brown and gray.

**ABUNDANCE & DISTRIBUTION:** Abundant to occasional East Florida, Bahamas, Caribbean.

**HABITAT & BEHAVIOR:** Inhabit most deep water environments, from patch reefs to deep slopes, canyons, crevices and along walls. Prefer clear water areas with some current. Most common below 60 feet. Polyps often extended, especially when there is water movement.

## WIDE-MESH SEA FAN
*Gorgonia mariae*
SUBORDER:
Holaxonia
FAMILY:
Gorgoniidae

SIZE: Colony height
6 - 12 in.
DEPTH: 3 - 156 ft.

### Yellow Variety

## DEEPWATER SEA FAN
*Iciligorgia schrammi*
SUBORDER:
Scleraxonia
FAMILY:
Anthothelidae

SIZE: Colony height
1 - 4 ft.
DEPTH: 35 - 1200 ft.

*continued next page*

# Gorgonians

**Polyp Detail**

**VISUAL ID:** Form both slender branching and stout, rod-like colonies. Cone-shaped calyces protrude noticeably. Red stems with red calyces or red stems with yellow calyx rims or yellow to orange stems with reddish, violet or purple calyx rims; polyps white and somewhat translucent. (Stout, rod-like colonies similar to Brilliant Sea Fingers [next] distinguished by smooth rod surfaces.)

**ABUNDANCE & DISTRIBUTION:** Common to occasional South Florida, Bahamas, Caribbean.

**HABITAT & BEHAVIOR:** Inhabit wide range of moderate to deep environments, from patch reefs to sandy and rocky substrates to shaded areas under ledges, overhangs along deep walls.

**NOTE:** A small sample of photographed specimen was collected and visual identification confirmed by microscopic examination of spicules.

**Branch/Polyp Detail**

**DEEP WATER SEA FAN**
*continued from previous page*
**Colony with Polyps Extended**

**COLORFUL SEA ROD**
*Diodogorgia nodulifera*
SUBORDER:
Scleraxonia
FAMILY:
Anthothelidae

SIZE: 4 - 12 in.
DEPTH: 45 - 600 ft.

**Orange Stem, Reddish Calyx Variety**

# Gorgonians

**VISUAL ID:** Colonies usually form short, stout, smooth cylindrical rods; occasionally tall, with several branches. Bright red to pinkish red, orange and yellowish orange; polyps translucent white.

**ABUNDANCE & DISTRIBUTION:** Occasional East Florida. Not reported Bahamas or Caribbean.

**HABITAT & BEHAVIOR:** Inhabit current-swept areas with hard, rocky substrates. Tend to be red off North Florida and orange off South Florida.

**Polyp Detail**

**VISUAL ID:** Scraggly, bushy, occasionally fan-shaped colonies with relatively thin branches and long protruding calyces. Only gorgonian in South Florida, Bahamas and Caribbean (within safe diving limits) with both orange to red stems and polyps.

**ABUNDANCE & DISTRIBUTION:** Common Florida; occasional to uncommon Bahamas, Caribbean.

**HABITAT & BEHAVIOR:** In Florida inhabit moderate to deep patch reefs and rocky/sandy substrates; colonies often quite bushy (opposite). In Caribbean, tend to inhabit only deep water environments over 100 feet, especially under ledge overhangs and cave ceilings; colonies often in fan-like growth pattern (next page, right).

## BRILLIANT SEA FINGERS
*Titanideum frauenfeldii*
SUBORDER:
Scleraxonia
FAMILY:
Anthothelidae

SIZE: Colony height
3 in. - 2 ft.
DEPTH: 50 - 780 ft.

**Typical Rod-like
Colonies**

## RED POLYP OCTOCORAL
*Swiftia exserta*
SUBORDER:
Holaxonia
FAMILY:
Plexauridae

SIZE: Colony height
6 - 18 in.
DEPTH: 40 - 260 ft.

*continued next page*

# Gorgonians

**Polyp Detail**

**VISUAL ID:** Colonies form single, long, whip-like stalks that taper slightly from base to tip. Bright orange to orange-red to red; polyps white.

**ABUNDANCE & DISTRIBUTION:** Common to occasional East Florida, Bahamas, Caribbean.

**HABITAT & BEHAVIOR:** Inhabit deep, clear water environments, especially on steep slopes and walls. Attach to rocky substrate.

**Polyp Detail**

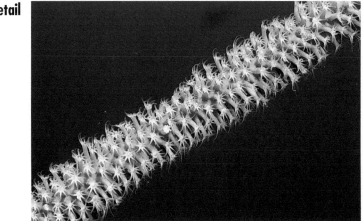

## RED POLYP OCTOCORAL
continued from
previous page
**Fan-like Growth
Pattern**

## DEVIL'S SEA WHIP
*Ellisella barbadensis*
SUBORDER:
Holaxonia
FAMILY:
Ellisellidae

**SIZE:** Colony height
2 - 8 ft.
Base diameter ¹/₄ - ¹/₂ in.
**DEPTH:** 65 - 1600 ft.

# Gorgonians

**VISUAL ID:** Tall, erect colonies branch dichotomously from short base stalks. Branches long, stiff, and whip-like. (Similar Bushy Sea Whips [next] occasionally grow upright, but are easily distinguished by their short branches that tend to rebranch several times.) Branches number from a few to over two dozen. Bright orange to orange-red to red; polyps white.

**ABUNDANCE & DISTRIBUTION:** Occasional Florida, Bahamas, Caribbean.

**HABITAT & BEHAVIOR:** Attach to rocky substrates in deep, clear water environments, especially on steep slopes and walls. In Caribbean most common below 100 feet, but along Florida Gulf Coast as shallow as 50 feet.

**SIMILAR SPECIES:** *E. grandis* may be indistinguishable underwater. However, the genus *Ellisella* needs revision before scientific accuracy in identifying and distinguishing species is possible.

**Polyp Detail**

**VISUAL ID:** Fan-shaped colonies, formed by some lateral branching off main stalks and profuse dichotomous rebranching, all in single planes. Bright orange to orange to red; polyps white.

**ABUNDANCE & DISTRIBUTION:** Occasional South Florida, Bahamas, Caribbean.

**HABITAT & BEHAVIOR:** Inhabit deep, clear water environments, especially under ledge overhangs, on cave ceilings, and along canyons, crevices and walls. Rare within safe diving limits.

## LONG SEA WHIP
*Ellisella elongata*
SUBORDER:
Holaxonia
FAMILY:
Ellisellidae

SIZE: Colony height
3 - 5 ft.
Base diameter $^1/_4$ - $^1/_2$ in.
DEPTH: 50 - 720 ft.

## ORANGE DEEP WATER FAN
*Nicella goreaui*
SUBORDER:
Holaxonia
FAMILY:
Ellisellidae

SIZE: Colony height
$^1/_2$ - 1$^1/_2$ ft.
DEPTH: 100 - 260 ft.

*continued next page*

# Gorgonians

**Polyp Detail**

**VISUAL ID:** Numerous short, stiff, whip-like branches and secondary branches extend from base stalks. (Similar Long Sea Whip [previous] distinguished by branches that are long and generally without secondary branches.) Branching and rebranching are both lateral and dichotomous. Bright orange to orange to red; polyps white.

**ABUNDANCE & DISTRIBUTION:** Common to occasional South Florida, Bahamas, Caribbean.

**HABITAT & BEHAVIOR:** Inhabit deep, clear water environments, especially under ledge overhangs, on cave ceilings, and along canyons, crevices and walls. Rarely grow upright like similar Long Sea Whip [previous page].

### ORANGE DEEP WATER FAN
*continued from previous page*
**Polyps Retracted**

### BUSHY SEA WHIP
*Nicella schmitti*
SUBORDER:
Holaxonia
FAMILY:
Ellisellidae

**Polyp Detail**
[far left]
**Bushy Branch Detail**
[near left]

SIZE: Colony height
1 - 2 ft.
Base diameter $^1/_4$ - $^1/_2$ in.
DEPTH: 65 - 220 ft.

# Gorgonians

**VISUAL ID:** Colonies form long, straight, stiff, moderately branched, whip-like stalks. Polyps in multiple rows along two sides. Calyces do not protrude when polyps are retracted. Stalks' color highly variable, including shades of lavender, violet, purple, red, orange and yellow; polyps translucent white.

**ABUNDANCE & DISTRIBUTION:** Common both coasts of Florida.

**HABITAT & BEHAVIOR:** Inhabit most environments, especially in areas with hard substrate and some sand.

**NOTE:** Small sample of pictured specimen was collected and visual identification confirmed by microscopic examination of spicules. Formerly classified *Lophogorgia*, which is no longer considered a separate genus.

**Orange Variety**

**Branch/Polyp Detail**

**COLORFUL SEA WHIP**
*Leptogorgia virgulata*
SUBORDER:
Holaxonia
FAMILY:
Gorgoniidae

SIZE: Colony height
$^1/_2$ - $1^1/_2$ ft.
DEPTH: 25 - 130 ft.

**Violet Variety**

# Gorgonians

**VISUAL ID:** Colonies thickly branched, generally in single planes. Branches somewhat flattened. Polyps alternate in rows along edges. Rows are separated by distinct grooves on older main branches. Calyces generally more prominent in older parts of colony. Branches orange to red, reddish purple and purple; polyps translucent to white.

**ABUNDANCE & DISTRIBUTION:** Common both coasts of Florida. Not known from Bahamas, Caribbean.

**HABITAT & BEHAVIOR:** Inhabit most environments, especially in areas with hard substrate and some sand.

**NOTE:** Small sample of pictured specimen was collected and visual identification confirmed by microscopic examination of spicules. Formerly classified *Lophogorgia*, which is no longer considered a separate genus.

**Branch Detail:
Polyps Extended**

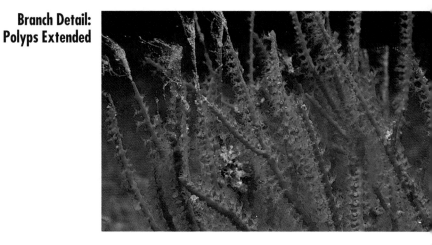

**VISUAL ID:** Small, openly pinnate branching colonies. Commonly branch in a single plane, but may be somewhat bushy. Low, blunt calyces in single rows along the two edges of outer branches; thicker branches have double rows. Branches orange-red to red to reddish purple; polyps translucent white.

**ABUNDANCE & DISTRIBUTION:** Occasional Florida, southeastern and southern Caribbean. Not reported Bahamas or remainder of Caribbean.

**HABITAT & BEHAVIOR:** Inhabit most environments, especially in areas with hard substrate and some sand.

**NOTE:** Small sample of pictured specimen was collected and visual identification confirmed by microscopic examination of spicules. Formerly classified *Lophogorgia*, which is no longer considered a separate genus.

## REGAL SEA FAN
*Leptogorgia hebes*
SUBORDER:
Holaxonia
FAMILY:
Gorgoniidae

SIZE: Colony ¹/₂ - 1¹/₂ ft.
DEPTH: 25 - 130 ft.

## Branch Detail: Polyps Retracted

## CARMINE SEA SPRAY
*Leptogorgia miniata*
SUBORDER:
Holaxonia
FAMILY:
Gorgoniidae

SIZE: Colony 2 - 5 in.
DEPTH: 40 - 120 ft.

*continued next page*

**Branch Detail: Polyps Expanded**

**VISUAL ID:** Fan-shaped colonies with regular pinnate branching in a single plane. Branches stiff, widely spaced and somewhat enlarged at the tips. Hard, rough, prickly calyces, without terminal spikes are openly spaced and protrude noticeably. Branches brownish yellow to brownish orange to orange or red; polyps' tentacles translucent to white, centers yellowish to orange or red.

**ABUNDANCE & DISTRIBUTION:** Occasional both Florida coasts. Not reported Bahamas, Caribbean.

**HABITAT & BEHAVIOR:** Inhabit clear water, moderate to deep fore reef environments.

**SIMILAR SPECIES:** Five additional species of *Muricea* are described on pages 43-47.

**NOTE:** Small sample of pictured specimen was collected and visual identification confirmed by microscopic examination of spicules.

**Polyp Detail**

**CARMINE SEA SPRAY**
*continued from previous page*
**Bushy Colony**

**PINNATE SPINY SEA FAN**
*Muricea pendula*
SUBORDER:
Holaxonia
FAMILY:
Plexauridae

SIZE: Colony height
8 - 18 in.
DEPTH:40 - 120 ft.

**Branch Detail:
Note Prickly Calyces**

77

# Gorgonians

**VISUAL ID:** Lateral branching colonies generally in a single plane; larger colonies tend to be somewhat bushy. Branches of living specimens are yellow-brown to reddish brown to grayish red. Normally extended polyps bright red to pink, often with white centers.

**ABUNDANCE & DISTRIBUTION:** Common off North Florida Atlantic coast. Additional distribution within safe diving limits not reported. Deep dwelling specimens reported from Dry Tortugas and eastern Caribbean.

**HABITAT & BEHAVIOR:** Inhabit areas of hard substrate.

**NOTE:** Samples of pictured specimens were collected and identification made by microscopic examination of spicules.

**Colonies with Partially Retracted and Retracted Polyps**

## WHITE EYE SEA SPRAY
*Thesea nivea*
SUBORDER:
Holaxonia
FAMILY:
Gorgoniidae

SIZE: Colony 6 - 18 in.
DEPTH: 75 - 1,200 ft.

**Bushy Colony**

**Polyp Detail:
Note Branch Color**

**Polyp Detail,
Without White
Centers**
[far left]

**Polyp Detail,
With White
Centers**
[near left]

**VISUAL ID:** Colonies thickly branched, generally in single planes, often fan-shaped. Polyps usually extended and protrude dramatically from relatively thin stems. Polyps bright yellow to yellow-gold; stems yellowish to tan or brown.

**ABUNDANCE & DISTRIBUTION:** Common Northwest Caribbean. Not reported remainder of Carribean, Florida or Bahamas.

**HABITAT & BEHAVIOR:** Inhabit deep reefs, especially along drop-offs and walls. Most common in protected areas, under ledge overhangs, wall undercuts, narrow canyons and crevices; occasionally exposed on reef tops.

**NOTE:** Small sample of pictured specimen was collected and microscopic examination confirmed this as a previously uncollected, undescribed species. Species first described in 1990 from locations off Brazil, between 22-100 feet. Previously unknown in Caribbean.

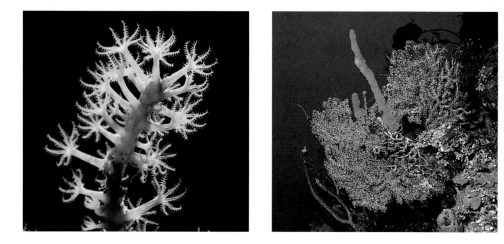

**VISUAL ID:** Colonies form rigid stalks with large, prominent, white to translucent polyps. Stalks tipped with single polyp; below, secondary (daughter) polyps grow at intervals of about 3/8 inch. Bright red to pink. Polyps usually extended. Stalks often encrusted and/or overgrown with algae, sponge and other organisms.

**ABUNDANCE & DISTRIBUTION:** Uncommon Bahamas, eastern Caribbean. Not reported Florida, West or Northwest Caribbean.

**HABITAT & BEHAVIOR:** Inhabit deep shaded areas, such as narrow canyon walls and caves. Prefer areas regularly swept with current.

**NOTE:** Photographed specimen was collected and visual identification confirmed by examination with scanning electron microscope. This species' closest relative is *S. rubra* from the Indian Ocean. Previously classified in the genus *Telesto*.

### GOLDEN SEA SPRAY
*Heterogorgia uatumani*
SUBORDER:
Holaxonia
FAMILY:
Plexauridae

SIZE: Colony ¹/₂ - 1 ft.
DEPTH: 75 - 150 ft.

### Small Colony

### Polyp Detail
[far left]
### Fan-shaped Colony
[near left]

### RIGID RED TELESTO
*Stereotelesto corallina*
FAMILY:
Clavulariidae
SUBFAMILY:
Telestinae

SIZE: Height ³/₄ - 2 in.
DEPTH: 75 - 600 ft.

*continued next page*

# Gorgonians

**VISUAL ID:** Colonies form dense clusters of tangled, branched stems with large, prominent, white polyps. Stems tipped with single polyps; below, secondary (daughter) polyps grow in pairs or groups of three at about the same level. White to pale pink stalks have eight longitudinal grooves. Polyps usually extended. Stems often encrusted and/or overgrown with algae, sponge and other organisms.

**ABUNDANCE & DISTRIBUTION:** Occasional South Florida, Bahamas, Caribbean.

**HABITAT & BEHAVIOR:** Considered a fouling organism. Can be abundant in shallow, rocky areas and under docks. In deeper water common on shipwrecks — often the first octocorallian to inhabit new wrecks/artificial reefs. Uncommon on reefs and walls.

**NOTE:** Previously classified in the genus *Telesto*.

**VISUAL ID:** Colonies form clusters of branched stems with large, prominent, white polyps. Stems tipped with single polyp; below, secondary (daughter) polyps extend from all sides. Yellow to orange to pale red stalks have eight longitudinal grooves. Polyps usually extended. Stems often encrusted and/or overgrown with algae, sponge and other organisms.

**ABUNDANCE & DISTRIBUTION:** Occasional Florida's Atlantic coast from West Palm Beach northward to Carolinas. Not reported Bahamas, Caribbean.

**HABITAT & BEHAVIOR:** Inhabit areas of rocky outcroppings and hard rubble, also attach to wrecks.

**SIMILAR SPECIES:** Red Telesto, *T. sanguinea*, is bright coral red, 75-350 feet, both Florida coasts and Keys.

**NOTE:** Photographed specimen was collected and visual identification confirmed by microscopic examination.

## WHITE TELESTO
*Carijoa riisei*
FAMILY:
Clavulariidae
SUBFAMILY:
Telestinae

**Colony Encrusting Shipwreck**
[far left]

**Polyp Detail**
[near left]

SIZE: Height 2 - 10 in.
DEPTH: 0 - 180 ft.

## ORANGE TELESTO
*Telesto fruticulosa*
FAMILY:
Clavulariidae
SUBFAMILY:
Telestinae

SIZE: Height 2 - 6 in.
DEPTH: 75 - 300 ft.

*continued next page*

# Gorgonians

**VISUAL ID:** Thick, rubbery, tree-like trunk and branches. Clusters or tufts of polyps on branch tips. Embedded skeletal elements (spicules) visible in translucent trunk and branches. Pastel shades of orange to yellow, gold and pink.

**ABUNDANCE & DISTRIBUTION:** Rare within safe diving limits Bahamas, Caribbean. Pictured specimens were observed at 120 feet, Cay Sal Banks, Bahamas.

**HABITAT & BEHAVIOR:** Inhabit deep drop-offs, often under ledge overhangs, wall undercuts and other shaded areas.

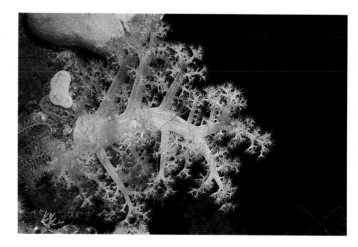

**ORANGE TELESTO**
*continued from
previous page*
**Polyp Detail**

**PASTEL SOFT CORAL**
*Neospongodes
portoricensis*
ORDER:
Alcyonacea
FAMILY:
Nephtheidae

SIZE: Height $^1/_2$ - 1 ft.
DEPTH: 120 - 1650 ft.

# Class Anthozoa
# Subclass Hexacorallia

(Hex-ah-core-AL-ee-uh/Gr. & L. six and coral animal)

Hexacorallian polyps are generally smooth and tubular with tentacles in multiples of six. The subclass has six orders that separate anemones, zoanthids, corallimorphs, tube-dwelling anemones (see REEF CREATURE Identification), black corals (see Identification Group 4), and stony corals.

## STONY CORALS

**Order Scleractinia** (Scler-ak-TIN-ee-uh/L. & Gr. hard and ray)

Stony corals, often called hard corals, are the basic building blocks of tropical coral reefs. These animals (polyps) secrete calcium carbonate to form hard cups, called **corallites**, that provide protection for their soft delicate bodies. In tropical waters most species grow colonially, joining their corallites to produce a substantial structure. Colonies increase in size by asexual budding of additional polyps and successive generations overgrowing one another. The maximum size, shape and design of these structures vary from species to species. Many species can be identified by simply observing the overall structure. Other species, however, grow in similar patterns and require a closer, more detailed inspection of the individual corallites or other parts of the structure before a positive species identification can be made.

Colonial corals that contribute substantial amounts of calcium carbonate (limestone) to the reef structure, are called hermatypic or reef-building corals. They live within a narrow temperature range, generally between 70 and 85 degrees Fahrenheit, although most species will survive for short periods, and a few hearty species will grow, in temperatures from 61 to 97 degrees. Non-reef-building corals, called ahermatypic, are usually small, occasionally solitary and without substantial skeletons.

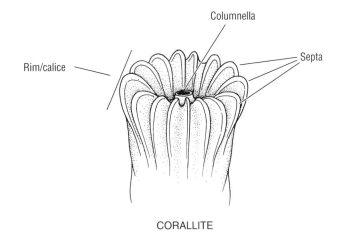

CORALLITE

To assist in the visual identification of stony corals, the 72 species identified in this text have been arranged by the shape and/or appearance of the colony, rather than the traditional scientific family groupings. This method has, in most cases, kept members of the same genus together. The groupings are: (1) **Branching & Pillar Corals**; (2) **Encrusting, Mound & Boulder Corals**; (3) **Brain Corals**; (4) **Leaf, Plate & Sheet Corals**; (5) **Fleshy Corals**; (6) **Flower & Cup Corals**.

BRANCHING & PILLAR CORAL

ENCRUSTING

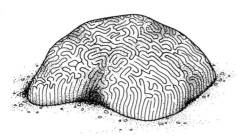

BRAIN CORAL

LEAF, PLATE & SHEET CORALS

FLESHY CORAL

FLOWERING & CUP CORALS

87

The shape and size of corallites are unique and distinguish species. When colonial structures are similar, close examination of the corallites' structural parts may be required before a correct identification can be made. Generally **corallites** are constructed in a circular pattern, but occasionally they are uneven, oval, Y-shaped or join to form elongated **valleys** and **ridges**. The tubular structure of the polyp's body has a number of vertical infolds on the surface. Calcium carbonate deposited in these folds form thin, upright, radiating plates or ridges, called **septa**. Often the number and structure of the septa are distinctive of species. The corallite structures of many species project above the overall colony forming distinctive rims, called **calices**, which can also be indicative of species. The central axis of a corallite called the **columella** is below the **polyp mouth**.

The polyps of most Caribbean stony corals are usually retracted into their corallites during the day. At night they extend both their bodies and tentacles for feeding, giving the colony a dramatically different appearance. Their nocturnal form, however, is not useful in determining species. Consequently, only occasional pictures of a coral's nighttime appearance are included in this text.

Reef building corals (hermatypic) typically get their color from single-celled algae, called zooxanthellae (zo-zan-THEL-ee), that live in the polyp's tissues. This symbiotic relationship is not fully understood, but clearly the biological processes of each is useful to the other. Most importantly, the zooxanthellae seem to stimulate or aid the secretion of calcium carbonate. Without the algae, coral growth slows dramatically and the polyps' tissues are transparent to translucent revealing the white calcium carbonate skeleton beneath. What causes the algae to be expelled from the polyps' tissues is currently a matter of great scientific concern and debate. It is known that this process, called bleaching, takes place during times of stress; for example, after hurricanes and when water temperatures are unusually high. When conditions return to normal, corals that are bleached regain their zooxanthellae. However, corals cannot live for prolonged periods without the algae. Continued stressful conditions are therefore cause for apprehension. The current fear is that global warming is causing the abnormally high incidence of bleaching and that this may ultimately affect the diversity of corals found on reefs. Non-reef-building corals (ahermatypic) may or may not have zooxanthellae, in which case pigments of their own become prominent. Orange Cup Coral is an example.

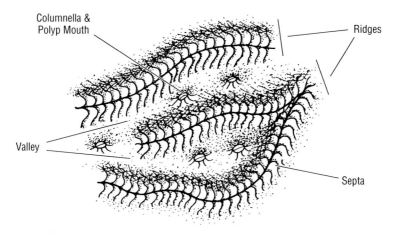

Columnella &
Polyp Mouth

Ridges

Valley

Septa

RIDGE-VALLEY

## BLACK-BAND DISEASE
*Phormidium coralyticum*

PHYLUM:
Cyanophyta

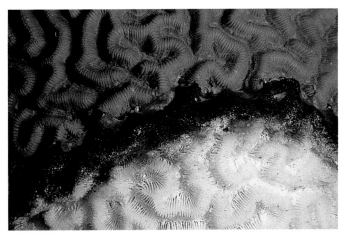

SIZE: Band Width
$^1/_4$ - $^1/_2$ in.
DEPTH: 3-60 ft.

**VISUAL ID:** Black to dark brown algal band composed of tightly woven filaments across coral colony. Coral polyps are killed as the band advances leaving only white limestone skeleton behind.

**ABUNDANCE & DISTRIBUTION:** Occasional South Florida, Bahamas, Caribbean.

**HABITAT & BEHAVIOR:** Attacks several species of shallow-water, hermatypic stony corals, eventually killing the entire colony. Research indicates it is a natural phenomenon and not the result of pollution.

# Branching & Pillar Corals

**VISUAL ID:** Colonies form antler-like racks of cylindrical branches that often grow in great tangles. Surface covered with small, protruding, tubular corallites. Brown to yellow-brown with a single, white terminal corallite. Fragile.

**ABUNDANCE & DISTRIBUTION:** Abundant to common Bahamas, Caribbean; occasional to uncommon South Florida.

**HABITAT & BEHAVIOR:** Prefer shallow to intermediate depths between 10-60 feet in clear, calm water. Most commonly on reefs, but colonies may grow separately on open clean areas of sand. Often form dense thickets with only outer branches living; the dead interior branches are usually encrusted with algae. Rapidly growing coral, under optimum conditions can grow five to six inches per year. Polyps usually retracted during day.

**VISUAL ID:** Colonies form antler-like racks of cylindrical branches. Often toward the tips of large branches a spray of shorter branches fuses forming flattened ends similar to Elkhorn Coral [next]; however, the individual branches of the spray remain evident. Surface covered with small, protruding, tubular corallites. Brown to yellow-brown with single, white terminal corallites. Fragile. (Note comparison in photograph, Fused Staghorn on left and Elkhorn on right.)

**ABUNDANCE & DISTRIBUTION:** Uncommon South Florida, Bahamas, Caribbean.

**HABITAT & BEHAVIOR:** Prefer areas of surge, on fore reefs between 2-12 feet. Rapidly growing coral, under optimum conditions can grow five to six inches per year. Polyps usually retracted during day.

**NOTE:** Some scientists believe this is an intermediate growth form between Staghorn and Elkhorn Corals.

## STAGHORN CORAL
*Acropora cervicornis*
SUBORDER:
Astrocoeniina
FAMILY:
Acroporidae

SIZE: Colony 1 - 8 ft.
Branch diameter
$^3/_4$ - $1^1/_4$ in.
DEPTH: 1 - 160 ft.

### Colonies Cover
### Large Area

**orallite Detail**
far left]

**angled Colony**
**)ver Sand**
near left]

---

## FUSED STAGHORN
*Acropora prolifera*
SUBORDER:
Astrocoeniina
FAMILY:
Acroporidae

SIZE: Colony 1 - 4 ft.
Branch diameter
$^3/_4$ - $1^1/_4$ in.
DEPTH: 1 - 90 ft.

# Branching & Pillar Corals

**VISUAL ID:** Colonies form flattened branches resembling the horns of moose or elk Surface covered with small, protruding, tubular corallites. Brown to yellow-brown White terminal corallites give the edges of outer branches a white outline. Somewhat fragile, branches break if pressure is applied.

**ABUNDANCE & DISTRIBUTION:** Abundant to common Bahamas, Caribbean. Once abundant in Florida Keys, but now common to occasional.

**HABITAT & BEHAVIOR:** Prefer shallow areas where wave action causes constant water movement. Most common between 1-35 feet. Branches orient parallel to surge direction. Can cover acres of shallow bottom. One of the primary corals of shallow fringing reefs. Upper branches may become exposed at low tide. Rapidly growing coral, under optimum conditions can grow five to six inches per year. Polyps usually retracted during day.

**Shallow Water Colony: Note Thick Branches**

**VISUAL ID:** Colonies form thick encrustations over areas of dead coral and rock substrate. May have knobby projections. Extended polyps give colony soft, fuzz appearance. When polyps are retracted, small, pitted, polygonal corallites give colony porous appearance. Bluish to pale lilac and purple color of living colonies i distinctive; often appear blue in natural light.

**ABUNDANCE & DISTRIBUTION:** Occasional to uncommon Bahamas, Caribbean rare Bahamas, South Florida.

**HABITAT & BEHAVIOR:** Inhabit shallow, dead areas of older reefs. Often in back reef areas of sand, coral rubble and coral heads.

**NOTE:** Also commonly known as "Porous Coral."

## ELKHORN CORAL
*Acropora palmata*
SUBORDER:
Astrocoeniina
FAMILY:
Acroporidae

SIZE: **Colony** 3 - 12 ft.
Branch diameter
2 - 10 in.
**DEPTH:** 1 - 55 ft.

## BLUE CRUST CORAL
*Porites branneri*
SUBORDER:
Fungiida
FAMILY:
Poritidae

SIZE: Colony 2 - 6 in.
Branch diameter $^1/_2$ - 1 in.
**DEPTH:** 10 - 35 ft.

# Branching & Pillar Corals

**VISUAL ID:** Colonies form smooth branches, with embedded corallites. There are three forms. Forma *porites* has stout, irregular, stubby branches with blunt and often enlarged tips. Forma *divaricata* has finger-like, widely spaced branches that often divide near the tip. Forma *furcata* has finger-like, tightly compacted branches. Color ranges from beige to yellow-brown, brown, gray, and gray with purple overtones. F. *divaricata* and *furcata* are fragile, while f. *porites* breaks only under pressure.

**ABUNDANCE & DISTRIBUTION:** Common to abundant South Florida, Bahamas, Caribbean.

**HABITAT & BEHAVIOR:** All three forms inhabit most reef environments and depths; however, f. *porites* is the most common form on moderate to deeper reefs; f. *divaricata* is most common on shallow, back reefs; f. *furcata* frequently forms large beds in shallow back reef areas. Polyps often extended during the day, giving colony a fuzzy appearance. Brittlestars, sea urchins and chitons often live among tightly compact branches of f. *furcata*.

**Large Colony
Clubtip Finger Coral
forma *porites***

**Rare Lavender Variety,
Thin Finger Coral
forma *divaricata***

**FINGER CORAL**
*Porites porites*
SUBORDER:
Fungiida
FAMILY:
Poritidae

**forma *porites***

SIZE: Colony 1 - 4 ft.
Branch diameter
¹/₂ - 1¹/₂ in.
DEPTH: 3 - 160 ft.

**Branched Finger Coral
forma *furcata***

**NOTE:** There is scientific controversy whether the three growth patterns are separate species or formas.

**Thin Finger Coral
forma *divaricata***

# Branching & Pillar Corals

**VISUAL ID:** Colonies form numerous, heavy, cylindrical spires that grow upward from an encrusting base mass. Light tan to golden brown and chocolate brown.

**ABUNDANCE & DISTRIBUTION:** Occasional to rare South Florida, Bahamas Caribbean.

**HABITAT & BEHAVIOR:** Inhabit flat and slightly sloping bottoms. Polyps are normally extended during the day, giving colony a fuzzy appearance. Fallen pillars often give rise to several new upward growing pillars.

**SIMILAR SPECIES:** An unusual growth pattern of Maze Coral [pg.128 ML] appears structurally similar, but the septa pattern of upright plates and ridge grooves is distinctive. Maze Pillar Coral, *Goreaugyra memorialis*, is distinguished by deep wide, meandering valleys between narrow, paired ridges separated by a shallow polyp bearing slit. Known only from Bahamas.

**Extended Polyp Detail**

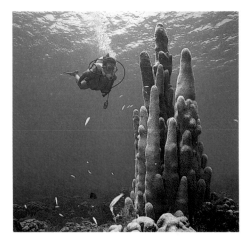

**PILLAR CORAL**
*Dendrogyra cylindrus*
SUBORDER:
Faviida
FAMILY:
Meandrinidae

SIZE: Colony 4 - 10 ft.
Pillar Diameter 3 - 5 in.
DEPTH: 4 - 65 ft.

**Fallen Colony
Growing New
Upright Pillars**

**Mature Colony**
[far left]
**Young Colony**
[near left]

**VISUAL ID:** Colonies form small, densely branching clumps in shallow water. Deeper, in depths generally over 65 feet, branching becomes more widely spaced. Branches have fine ridges running their length, and each ends with a single corallite. Tan to golden brown and dark brown. Fragile.

**ABUNDANCE & DISTRIBUTION:** Common to occasional Florida, Bahamas, Caribbean.

**HABITAT & BEHAVIOR:** Most commonly inhabit shallow areas of high sedimentation, such as Turtle Grass beds [pg.191]. Rarely on clear water reefs. Much of the colony is often dead, and may be covered with sediment, with only polyps at tips of outer branches living.

**NOTE:** Also commonly known as "Ivory Tube Coral."

**Deep Water
Variety**

**VISUAL ID:** Colonies form large, bushy or tree-like structures. Colony base (trunk) can be quite thick, branches long and tapering. Only corallites' rims protrude from colony. (Similar Diffuse Ivory Bush Coral, Delicate Bush Ivory Coral and Large Ivory Coral [next three species] distinguished by prominently protruding corallites.) Yellowish brown. Thin branch tips fragile.

**ABUNDANCE & DISTRIBUTION:** Abundant West Florida. Absent East Florida, Bahamas, Caribbean.

**HABITAT & BEHAVIOR:** Inhabit areas of hard substrate.

**NOTE:** Photographed specimen collected and visual identification confirmed by magnified examination of corallites and structure.

## TUBE CORAL
*Cladocora arbuscula*
**SUBORDER:**
Faviida
**FAMILY:**
Faviidae

SIZE: Colony 1 - 6 in.
Corallite diameter ¹/₄ in.
DEPTH: 3 - 65 ft.

**Corallites Protruding from Sand in Turtle Grass Bed**

## ROBUST IVORY TREE CORAL
*Oculina robusta*
**SUBORDER:**
Faviida
**FAMILY:**
Oculinidae

SIZE: Colony 4 - 30 in.
Corallite diameter ¹/₄ in.
Branch diameter to 3 in.
DEPTH: 20 - 85 ft.

**VISUAL ID:** Colonies form small clumps of thin branches. Branches may occasionally cross and fuse. Corallites protrude prominently from sides of branches. Branch diameter, corallite diameter and length all nearly equal. Cream to white. Fragile. Ahermatypic.

**ABUNDANCE & DISTRIBUTION:** Uncommon West Florida; rare East Florida. Not reported Bahamas, Caribbean.

**HABITAT & BEHAVIOR:** Inhabit areas of rocky rubble, shell hash under ledge overhangs and shipwrecks.

**NOTE:** Photographed specimen collected (USNM91649) and visual identification confirmed by magnified examination of corallites and structure.

---

**VISUAL ID:** Colonies form densely branched, thicket-like clumps. Branches tend to be short, are often crooked and bear numerous raised corallites. Yellow-brown, but often encrusted with organisms of different color. Somewhat fragile.

**ABUNDANCE & DISTRIBUTION:** Abundant to occasional Florida; common to occasional Bahamas; occasional to rare Caribbean. Absent around some islands, especially in northwest and southern Caribbean.

**HABITAT & BEHAVIOR:** Generally inhabit shallow water areas of high sedimentation, including sloping solid bottoms, reefs, back reefs and lagoons. Often attach to old shipwrecks. Much of the colony is often dead, and may be covered with sediment. Rarely deeper than 40 feet.

**SIMILAR SPECIES:** Ivory Tree Coral, *O. valenciennesi*, distinguished by longer, more tree-like branches, corallite rims low, often sunken into the branch structure. Common in Bermuda; rare or absent Florida, Bahamas, Caribbean.

**Colony with Branches Lacking Zooxanthellae and Others with Lavender Pigmentation**

### DELICATE IVORY BUSH CORAL
*Oculina tenella*
SUBORDER:
Faviida
FAMILY:
Oculinidae

SIZE: Colony 1 - 4 in.
Corallite diameter ¹/₈ in.
Branch diameter less than ¹/₄ in.
DEPTH: 60 - 250 ft.

### DIFFUSE IVORY BUSH CORAL
*Oculina diffusa*
SUBORDER:
Faviida
FAMILY:
Oculinidae

SIZE: Colony 1 - 12 in.
Corallite diameter ¹/₄ in.
Branch diameter less than ¹/₂ in.
DEPTH: 3 - 75 ft.

**Colony on Dark Interior Ceiling of Shipwreck Lacks Zooxanthellae**

*(USNM 92075)*

101

# Branching & Pillar Corals

**VISUAL ID:** Colonies form large, tangled clumps of long crooked branches. Corallites extend prominently from raised mounds on branches' sides, except on smaller branches and near branch tips. Yellowish brown; without zooxanthellae, white to lavender. Thinner branches fragile.

**ABUNDANCE & DISTRIBUTION:** Uncommon Florida; rare to absent Bahamas, Caribbean.

**HABITAT & BEHAVIOR:** Wide range of habitats from shallow reefs to deep, rocky outcroppings. Rare in shallow water, most common between 150-300 feet. Small colonies not uncommon, 75-125 feet, central and northern Florida Atlantic Coast.

**NOTE:** Photographed specimens collected (USNM 91669) and visual identification confirmed by magnified examination of corallites and structure.

**Small Colony**

*(USNM 91670)*

**VISUAL ID:** Colonies form densely packed clumps of small pencil-sized branches with blunt tips. Colonies appear fuzzy when polyps are extended. Creamy to bright yellow. Fragile.

**ABUNDANCE & DISTRIBUTION:** Common South Florida, Bahamas, Caribbean.

**HABITAT & BEHAVIOR:** Generally inhabit deeper, clear water, outer reefs. Occasionally in shallower water with some sedimentation and water movement. Often cover considerable area of flat bottom. Polyps are generally extended.

**SIMILAR SPECIES:** Pointed Pencil Coral, *M. asperula*, branches tapered rather than blunt. Deep dwelling coral known primarily from southern Caribbean.

**NOTE:** Also commonly known as "Small Finger Coral" and "Branching Coral."

## LARGE IVORY CORAL
*Oculina varicosa*
SUBORDER:
Faviida
FAMILY:
Oculinidae

SIZE: Colony 3 - 24 in.
Corallite diameter ¹/₄ in.
Branch diameter ¹/₂ - 2 in.
DEPTH: 15 - 300 ft.

### Branch Detail: Note Corallites' Swollen Bases

## YELLOW PENCIL CORAL
*Madracis mirabilis*
SUBORDER:
Astrocoeniina
FAMILY:
Pocilloporidae

SIZE: Colony 5 in. - 4 ft.
Branch diameter ¹/₄ - ³/₈ in.
DEPTH: 3 - 190 ft.

*continued next page*

**103**

# Branching & Pillar Corals

## Small Colony, Polyps Extended

**VISUAL ID:** Colonies form densely packed clumps of thick, relatively short branches with blunt and occasionally expanded and double-lobed tips. Colonies appear fuzzy when polyps are extended. Tan to yellow-brown, yellow-green, brown and green; polyp's mouth yellow. Not fragile, but will break under moderate pressure.

**ABUNDANCE & DISTRIBUTION:** Common to occasional South Florida, Bahamas, Caribbean.

**HABITAT & BEHAVIOR:** Inhabit deep outer reefs, often on outcroppings and ledges along walls.

**NOTE:** Also commonly known as "Branching Cactus Coral."

## Corallite Detail

## YELLOW PENCIL CORAL
*continued from previous page*

### Branch Detail: Note Blunt Tips

## EIGHT-RAY FINGERCORAL
*Madracis formosa*

SUBORDER:
Astrocoeniina
FAMILY:
Pocilloporidae

SIZE: Colony 1 - 5 ft.
Branch diameter ³/₄ - 1¹/₄ in.
DEPTH: 60 - 200 ft.

### Small Colony

# Encrusting, Mound & Boulder Corals

**VISUAL ID:** Thinly encrusting, small colonies, often with raised, tightly bunched lobes or knobs. Surface densely covered with separated, small, protruding corallites. Often green, but vary from yellow-brown to violet-brown, tan and gray.

**ABUNDANCE & DISTRIBUTION:** Common South Florida, Bahamas, Caribbean.

**HABITAT & BEHAVIOR:** Inhabit most reef environments. Usually develop lobes and knobs when growing in the open and exposed to bright light. Form irregular encrustations in shaded, protected areas of reef, under ledge overhangs and on deep walls.

**NOTE:** Encrusting variety is visually indistinguishable from Encrusting Star Coral *M.pharensis* forma *luciphila* [next], but usually can be identified by habitat. Positive identification requires magnified examination of specimen sample. Ten-Ray Star Coral has ten primary septa, while Encrusting Star Coral has ten primary and ten secondary septa and small lobes around the columella. A rare similar species, Six-ray Star Coral, *M. senaria*, has only six primary septa. Identification of pictured specimens was confirmed by examination of small collected samples. Also commonly known as "Encrusting Madracis" and "Green Cactus Coral."

**Large Encrusting Colony on Deep Wall**

### TEN-RAY STAR CORAL
*Madracis decactis*
SUBORDER:
Astrocoeniina
FAMILY:
Pocilloporidae

SIZE: Colony 1 - 6 in.
Lobe diameters about 1 in.
DEPTH: 5 - 130 ft.

**Corallite Detail
Knobby Variety**

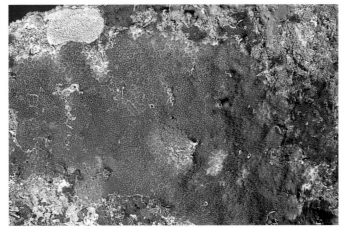

**Colony Encrusting
the Underside of
Ledge Overhang**

# Encrusting, Mound & Boulder Corals

**VISUAL ID:** Colonies grow in two forms. Forma *pharensis* [right] is either thinly encrusting, spreading in long ribbons, or may form numerous small knobs. May be shades of cream, yellow, pale green, dull red, pink or lavender. Ahermatypic. Forma *luciphila* is thickly encrusting and may have a smooth or somewhat lumpy surface. Green to brown or gray. Hermatypic.

**ABUNDANCE & DISTRIBUTION:** Occasional Bahamas, Caribbean. Not reported Florida.

**HABITAT & BEHAVIOR:** Forma *pharensis* grows in dark areas, such as the underside of plate corals and cave ceilings; most common deeper than 60 feet. Forma *luciphila* generally grows in exposed, well lighted areas of reef, often encrusting the sheer faces of cliffs, canyon and drop-off walls; may be as shallow as six feet.

**NOTE:** Forma *luciphila* is visually indistinguishable from the encrusting variety of Ten-ray Star Coral [see previous note]. There is evidence suggesting that Encrusting Star Coral is a form of Ten-ray Star Coral. (See D. Fenner, *Bull.Mar.Sci.*, in press 1992.) Identification confirmed by examination of collected samples.

**Cave Star Coral forma *pharensis*, Detail Knobby Variety**

**Encrusting Star Coral forma *luciphila*, Encrusting Shallow Reef**

**STAR CORAL**
*Madracis pharensis*
SUBORDER:
Astrocoeniina
FAMILY:
Pocilloporidae

**forma *pharensis***

SIZE: Colony 1 - 6 in.
DEPTH: 6 - 450 ft.

**Cave Star Coral
forma *pharensis*,
Knobby Variety
on Deep Cave Ceiling**

**Encrusting Star Coral
forma *luciphila*,
Encrusting Shallow
Canyon Wall**

# Encrusting, Mound & Boulder Corals

**VISUAL ID:** Colonies form relatively smooth domes or boulders; occasionally encrust substrate. Circular, upper rims of calices darker than surrounding area. Brownish-cream to tan, brown and gray. Corallites may be widely spaced or closely compacted. When approached or touched appear to "blush" a lighter shade. (This is caused by the rapid retraction of its tiny, normally extended polyps.)

**ABUNDANCE & DISTRIBUTION:** Occasional South Florida, Bahamas, Caribbean.

**HABITAT & BEHAVIOR:** Inhabit most reef environments. Numerous reddish Blushing Star Coral Fanworms [*Reef Creature ID*, pg. 141] often associate with this species. When present, they retract with the polyps, enhancing the blushing effect.

**NOTE:** Visual identification of pictured specimens confirmed by collection of small samples and magnified examination of corallites.

**Encrusting Variety, Polyps Extended**

**Tightly Compacted Polyp Variety: Note Fanworms**

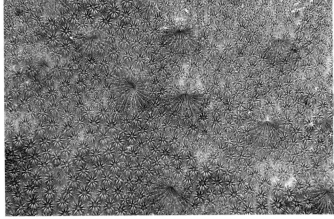

## BLUSHING STAR CORAL

*Stephanocoenia*
*mechelinii*

SUBORDER:
Astrocoeniina
FAMILY:
Astrocoeniinae

SIZE: Colony $1/2$ - $2^1/_2$ ft.
DEPTH: 10 - 130 ft.

**Detail: Encrusting Variety, Polyps Retracted**

*(USNM 92955)*

**Boulder Variety with Tightly Compacted Polyps**

*(USNM 92954)*

# Encrusting, Mound & Boulder Corals

**VISUAL ID:** Colonies grow in four configurations (morphotypes) that were origianlly described as three separate species. Later, because of similarity in corallite structure, most scientists concluded that the morphytes were variations of the same species, due to different environmental conditions. They were synonymized as one species, Bolder Star Coral, *M. annalaris.*

Recent evidence (Sibling species of *M. annalaris,* E. Weil & N. Knowlton, Bull. Mar. Sci. May 94), however, strongly indicates there are three and possibly more species. The redescribed scientific names and this author's suggested common names follow. (1) **Lobed Star Coral**, [right], grow in clusters of long, thick columns with enlarged, dome-like tops. Living polyps are restricted to the upper portions of the column, while lower parts are often bioeroded and fouled with algae. Surfaces are usually smooth with close, uniformly distributed and evenly extended corallites. (2) **Mountainous Star Coral**, *M. faveolata*, grow in large, massive mounds [below left] and sheets with skirt-like edges [right middle]. Often cone-like bumps form on the surface that are usually arranged in vertical rows. Surfaces are usually smooth with uniformly distributed and evenly extended corallites. (3) **Bolder Star Coral***M. franksi* [right bottom], grow in irregular mounds and encrustations with corallites. Often small clusters of polyps are without zooxanthellae. (4) One and possibly two deepwater morphyte/s of flattened plates (some smooth, others lumpy), often stacked in shingle-like fashion [below right], require further investigation to determine the appropriate classification. All types vary in shades of green to brown, yellow-brown and gray.

**ABUNDANCE & DISTRIBUTION:** Common to abundant South Florida, Bahamas, Caribbean.

**HABITAT & BEHAVIOR:** Growth configurations (1), (2) and (3) inhabit most reef environments and together are often the predominate coral between 20-75 feet. Of the three, (2) is generally the most common. Flattened plate morphyte (4) usually grow at depths greater than 80 feet.

## BOULDER STAR CORAL
*Montastrea annularis*
SUBORDER:
Faviida
FAMILY:
Faviidae

**(1) Lobed Star Coral**

SIZE: Colony 1 - 10 ft.
Corallites about $^1/_8$ in.
DEPTH: 6 - 130 ft.

**(2) Mountainous Star Coral**
*Montastrea faveolata*
**(3) Boulder Star Coral**
*Montastrea franksi*
[below left]
**Colony and Corallite Detail,
Note Occasional Polyps
without Zooxanthellae**
[below right]
**(1) Mountainous Star Coral**
[below far left]
**(4) Flatten Plate Morphyte**
[below near left]

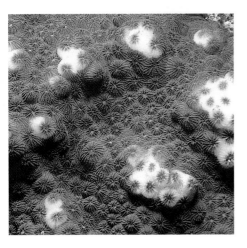

# Encrusting, Mound & Boulder Corals

**VISUAL ID:** Colonies usually form massive boulders and domes, but occasionally develop into plates or sheets, especially in deep water. Surface is covered with distinctive, blister-like corallites. Shades of green, brown, yellow-brown and gray. Occasionally fluoresce red or orange. (Fluorescence is not visible when lit by a hand light or strobe.)

**ABUNDANCE & DISTRIBUTION:** Common to abundant South Florida, Bahamas, Caribbean.

**HABITAT & BEHAVIOR:** Inhabit most reef environments and are often the predominant coral between 40-100 feet. Polyps are generally retracted during the day, but extend prominently at night.

**NOTE:** Also commonly known as "Large Star Coral."

**Reef Top Colony**

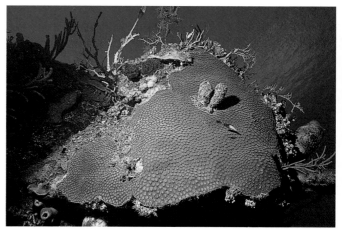

**Extended Polyp Detail**

## GREAT STAR CORAL
*Montastraea cavernosa*
SUBORDER:
Faviida
FAMILY:
Faviidae

SIZE: Colony 2 - 8 ft.
Corallites $^1/_4$ - $^1/_2$ in.
DEPTH: 6 - 300 ft.

**Corallite Detail**

# Encrusting, Mound & Boulder Corals

**VISUAL ID:** Colonies form relatively smooth domes, occasionally with a few slight, irregular bulges on their surfaces. Corallite rims protrude noticeably, giving a blistered appearance. Cream to light tan; extended polyps light tan to brown.

**ABUNDANCE & DISTRIBUTION:** Common to occasional South Florida; uncommon Bahamas, Caribbean.

**HABITAT & BEHAVIOR:** Inhabit reefs from shallow to moderate depths.

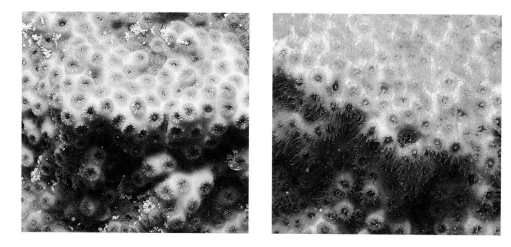

**VISUAL ID:** Colonies form lobated heads with irregular bulges on the surface. Corallite rims protrude noticeably and are irregularly spaced, some almost touching, while others may be separated by as much as their diameter. Usually yellow-brown, occasionally cream to tan; polyps dark brown.

**ABUNDANCE & DISTRIBUTION:** Abundant to occasional Florida; occasional to rare Bahamas, Caribbean.

**HABITAT & BEHAVIOR:** Inhabit a wide range of underwater environments from areas of high sedimentation, including back reefs, lagoons and Turtle Grass beds [pg. 191] to deep outer reefs. Can tolerate cool water; grow as far north as North Carolina where winter water temperatures may fall below 50°F.

**NOTE:** Also commonly known as "Stump Coral," "Lobed Star Coral" and "Eyed Coral."

## SMOOTH STAR CORAL
*Solenastrea bournoni*
SUBORDER:
Faviida
FAMILY:
Faviidae

SIZE: Colony 4 - 18 in.
DEPTH: 5 - 60 ft.

**Colony in Natural Light**
[right]

**Corallite Detail**
[far left]
**Polyp Detail**
[left]

## KNOBBY STAR CORAL
*Solenastrea hyades*
SUBORDER:
Faviida
FAMILY:
Faviidae

SIZE: Colony 3 in. - 2 ft.
DEPTH: 2 - 60 ft.

*continued next page*

# Encrusting, Mound & Boulder Corals

**VISUAL ID:** Colonies form rounded heads, domes and flattened plates. Corallites protrude perceptibly (up to one-quarter inch) and are usually elliptical or circular and occasionally Y-shaped. Cream to yellow and brown.

**ABUNDANCE & DISTRIBUTION:** Common Bahamas and Caribbean; occasional South Florida.

**HABITAT & BEHAVIOR:** Inhabit most reef environments. Most common between 30-80 feet. Rarely on reef crests.

**NOTE:** The flattened plate variety was formerly known as "Pancake Star Coral" and classified as a separate species, *D. stellaris*, but is now considered synonymous with *D. stokesii*. The rounded head variety is also commonly known as "Pineapple Star Coral."

**KNOBBY STAR CORAL**
*continued from previous page*
**Colony on Reef**

**Small Colony Detail**
[far left]
**Colony in Turtle Grass**
[near left]

---

**ELLIPTICAL STAR CORAL**
*Dichocoenia stokesii*
SUBORDER:
Faviida
FAMILY:
Meandrinidae

SIZE: Colony 4 - 15 in.
DEPTH: 12 - 225 ft.

**Flattened Plate Variety**

**Polyp/Corallite Detail**
[far left]
**Rounded Head Variety**
[near left]

# Encrusting, Mound & Boulder Corals

**VISUAL ID:** Usually form small hemispherical domes, but occasionally encrust small areas of substrate. Corallites are generally oval with protruding rims. Yellow to golden-brown and brown. (Easily distinguished from similar i.e. Elliptical Star Coral [previous] by colonies' smaller size and less pronounced protrusion of corallites.)

**ABUNDANCE & DISTRIBUTION:** Common Florida, Bahamas, Caribbean.

**HABITAT & BEHAVIOR:** Inhabit shallow reefs and rocky substrates. Most common between 10-40 feet.

**NOTE:** Also commonly known as "Star Coral."

---

**VISUAL ID:** Colonies encrust in shallow, surging water, but form rounded heads and domes in deeper water. Surface lumpy and covered with small, closely set corallites that give the colonies a porous appearance. Most commonly yellow to yellow-green or yellow-brown, occasionally beige to gray. Extended polyps give colonies a soft, fuzzy appearance.

**ABUNDANCE & DISTRIBUTION:** Abundant to common Florida, Bahamas, Caribbean.

**HABITAT & BEHAVIOR:** Inhabit all reef environments. Most common between 15-80 feet. Polyps usually extended.

**NOTE:** Also commonly known as "Yellow Porous Coral" and "Porous Coral."

**Polyp Detail**

## GOLFBALL CORAL
*Favia fragum*
SUBORDER:
Faviida
FAMILY:
Faviidae

SIZE: Colony 1 - 2 in.
DEPTH: 3 - 90 ft.

## MUSTARD HILL CORAL
*Porites astreoides*
SUBORDER:
Fungiida
FAMILY:
Poritidae

SIZE: Colony 6 in. - 2 ft.
DEPTH: 3 - 160 ft.

### Gray Variety

# Encrusting, Mound & Boulder Corals

**VISUAL ID:** Form rounded heads, boulders or domes. Surface covered with small, generally symmetrically round, pitted corallites. Light gray to golden-brown and brown; color uniform, corallites not dark at center. Young colonies are small, encrusting and difficult to distinguish from Lesser Starlet Coral [next] that have corallites less symmetrically round, more deeply pitted with dark centers, and more pronounced septa.

**ABUNDANCE & DISTRIBUTION:** Common Florida, Bahamas, Caribbean.

**HABITAT & BEHAVIOR:** Tend to inhabit shallow to moderate reefs, between 25-45 feet. Prefer clear water. Generally in protected areas of shallower reefs and all deeper reef environments. Usually deeper than similar Lesser Starlet [next].

**NOTE:** Also commonly known as "Smooth Starlet," "Round Starlet," and "Reef Starlet Coral."

**Corallite Detail
Comparison
Massive Starlet** [left]
**Lesser Starlet** [right]

**VISUAL ID:** Colonies usually form flat, encrusting plates, but occasionally grow in small, irregular and rounded domes. In shallow water they may form unattached, egg-shaped colonies that are rolled freely across the bottom by surge. Surface is covered with small, deep-pitted corallites that often appear "pinched-in". Usually whitish to light gray, occasionally light tan; center of corallite appears dark. Can be confused with Massive Starlet Coral [previous] that have corallites less steeply sloped, not dark toward center, and septa less pronounced.

**ABUNDANCE & DISTRIBUTION:** Common Florida, Bahamas, Caribbean.

**HABITAT & BEHAVIOR:** Inhabit flat rocky/sandy substrates, most commonly from low tide line to 20 feet, also shallow reefs and back reefs. Rarely below 30 feet. Can tolerate surge, sandy, silty conditions and temperature fluctuations. Usually shallower than similar Massive Starlet [previous].

**NOTE:** Also commonly known as "Rough Starlet," "Starlet Coral,"and "Shallow-water Starlet Coral."

### MASSIVE STARLET CORAL
*Siderastrea siderea*
SUBORDER:
Fungiida
FAMILY:
Siderastreidae

SIZE: Colony 1 - 6 ft.
DEPTH: 2 - 220 ft.

### Dome Variety

### LESSER STARLET CORAL
*Siderastrea radians*
SUBORDER:
Fungiida
FAMILY:
Siderastreidae

SIZE: Colony 4 - 12 in.
DEPTH: 0 - 90 ft.

123

# Brain Corals

**VISUAL ID:** Colonies form smoothly contoured plates to hemispherical domes. Long valleys are often connected and usually convoluted, except near colony's edge. Ridges evenly rounded, usually without a top groove, although occasionally with an extremely fine groove, especially near colony edge. (Similar Boulder Brain Coral [pg. 133] has a distinct groove on top of ridge. Similar Knobby Brain Coral [next] distinguished by sharply raised ridges and knobby surface.) Green to brown, yellow-brown and bluish gray; valleys often lighter or of contrasting color.

**ABUNDANCE & DISTRIBUTION:** Abundant to common Florida, Bahamas, Caribbean.

**HABITAT & BEHAVIOR:** Inhabit many marine environments, most common between 20-40 feet.

**NOTE:** Also commonly known as "Common Brain Coral," and "Smooth Brain Coral."

**VISUAL ID:** Colonies form hemispherical domes or encrust rocky substrate. Surfaces of colonies usually have numerous, irregular knobs, but occasionally form smooth low flattened domes. Ridges rise sharply and do not have a groove on top. (Similar Boulder Brain Coral [pg. 133] has a distinct groove on ridge top. Similar Symmetrical Brain Coral [previous] distinguished by evenly rounded ridges and smooth contour of colony.) Green to brown, yellow-brown and bluish gray; valleys often lighter or of contrasting color.

**ABUNDANCE & DISTRIBUTION:** Common Florida, Bahamas, Caribbean.

**HABITAT & BEHAVIOR:** Inhabit many shallow environments, including both seaward and lagoon sides of reefs, Turtle Grass beds [pg.191] and even on mangrove roots. Most common between 3-20 feet.

**NOTE:** Also commonly known as "Encrusting Brain Coral," "Sharp-hilled Brain Coral."

## SYMMETRICAL BRAIN CORAL
*Diploria strigosa*
SUBORDER:
Faviida
FAMILY:
Faviidae

SIZE: Colony 6 in. - 6 ft.
DEPTH: 3 - 130 ft.

## Hemispherical Head Variety

**Structural Detail:
Note Evenly
Rounded Ridges**
[far left]

**Encrusting Plate
Variety**
[near left]

## KNOBBY BRAIN CORAL
*Diploria clivosa*
SUBORDER:
Faviida
FAMILY:
Faviidae

SIZE: Colony 6 in. - 4 ft.
DEPTH: 3 - 135 ft.

*continued next page*

# Brain Corals

**Structural Detail:
Note Steep Ridges**

**VISUAL ID:** Colonies form hemispherical heads. Deep, often narrow, polyp bearing valleys are separated by broad ridges with wide, conspicuous trough-like grooves. Width and depth of grooves vary greatly from colony to colony, but are always obvious and usually make the ridge appear as two. Valleys are highly convoluted and often interconnected. Tan to yellow-brown to brown to brownish gray.

**ABUNDANCE & DISTRIBUTION:** Common to occasional South Florida, Bahamas, Caribbean.

**HABITAT & BEHAVIOR:** Inhabit seaward slope of reefs. Most common between 15-50 feet. Tentacle tips are often visible in the narrow valleys during the day.

**NOTE:** Also commonly known as "Depressed Brain Coral" and "Labyrinthine Brain Coral."

### KNOBBY BRAIN CORAL
*continued from previous page*
**Encrusting Variety**

---

### GROOVED BRAIN CORAL
*Diploria labyrinthiformis*
SUBORDER:
Faviida
FAMILY:
Faviidae

SIZE: Colony 1 - 4 ft.
DEPTH: 3 - 135 ft.

**Colony with Unusually Wide Groves**

**Structural Detail Comparing Different Grove Widths**
[far left & near left]

127

# Brain Corals

**VISUAL ID:** Colonies form both hemispherical heads and flattened plates; on occasion may encrust or form columns resembling Pillar Coral [pg. 97]. Ridges are created by smooth, widely separated, vertical plates (septa). There is a thin line along ridgetops where plates come together. Tan to yellow-brown and brown. There are two additional growth patterns; both form small elliptical colonies with cone-shaped undersides, often with short central stalks. Forma *danae* has a long, continuous, central valley and opposing side valleys. The central valley divides into two branches at the ends. Forma *brasiliensis* does not divide into two branches at ends and may not have a continuous central valley.

**ABUNDANCE & DISTRIBUTION:** Common to occasional South Florida, Bahamas, Caribbean.

**HABITAT & BEHAVIOR:** Inhabit most reef environments, especially on seaward reefs at depths between 25-75 feet. F. *danae* and f. *brasiliensis* often in areas of coral rubble and sand and may not be firmly attached to substrate.

**NOTE:** Also commonly known as "Butterprint Brain Coral" and "Tan Brain Coral."

**Brazilian Rose Coral
forma *brasiliensis*,
without
Central Valley**

### MAZE CORAL
*Meandrina meandrites*
SUBORDER:
Faviida
FAMILY:
Meandrinidae

SIZE: Colony 1 - 3 ft.
DEPTH: 2 - 240 ft.

**Plate-like Variety
at Night with
Polyps Extended**

**Pillar-like Variety**
[far left]
**Hemispherical Head
Variety**
[near left]

**Butterprint Rose Coral
forma *danae*:
Note Central Valley
and Branched Ends**

# Brain Corals

**VISUAL ID:** Colonies grow in two patterns. The most common builds small elliptical colonies with long, continuous central valley and several short side valleys. Cone-shaped underside, often with short central stalk. The second pattern builds hemispherical heads with winding valleys and ridges and flattish underside. Brown to yellow-brown, gray or green. Ridges and valleys often of contrasting shades or different color. (Distinguished from similar appearing forms of Maze Coral [previous] by less pronounced vertical plates.) Often young colonies form small circular to oval disks that can be confused with similar appearing Solitary Disk Coral [pg.157].

**ABUNDANCE & DISTRIBUTION:** Common to uncommon Florida, Bahamas, Caribbean.

**HABITAT & BEHAVIOR:** The small elliptical colonies tend to inhabit areas of coral rubble, sand and Turtle Grass, and are often unattached. The hemispherical heads tend to inhabit reefs along with other stony corals, and are attached.

**NOTE:** Some scientists consider the hemispherical head pattern a separate species or forma *mayori* and is commonly known as "Tortugas Rose Coral."

**Colony in Turtle Grass Bed, Tentacles Extended**

**Hemispherical Head Growth Pattern**

### ROSE CORAL
*Manicina areolata*
SUBORDER:
Faviida
FAMILY:
Faviidae

SIZE: Elliptical
Colony 2 - 6 in.
Hemispherical
Colony 4 - 8 in.
DEPTH: 2 - 200 ft.

**Hemispherical Head
Growth Pattern**

**Young Disk-shaped
Colony**

*(USNM 92082)*

131

# Brain Corals – Leaf, Plate & Sheet Corals

**VISUAL ID:** Colonies generally form large rounded domes, but also encrust, constructing large rounded plates. Surface covered with a convoluted system of ridges and valleys. A thin, but distinct groove runs along the ridgetops. There is also a thin, but noticeable line approximately halfway down the ridge where the slope decreases in angle and slants to form the valley. Typically the ridges are brown and valleys green, tan or whitish. Valleys are usually long and meandering, containing several polyps, but are occasionally closed, holding only one or two polyps.

**ABUNDANCE & DISTRIBUTION:** Common South Florida, Bahamas, Caribbean.

**HABITAT & BEHAVIOR:** Generally inhabit reef tops and seaward reef slopes. Most common between 20-80 feet. Polyps are extended only at night, their tentacles forming long meandering rows along the ridges (below).

**NOTE:** Colonies composed primarily of closed valleys were formerly known as "Closed-valley Brain Coral" and classified as a separate species, *C. breviserialis*, but are now synonymous with *C. natans*. Also commonly known as "Giant Brain Coral."

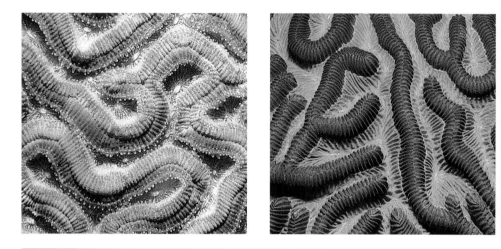

**VISUAL ID:** Colonies form thin plates that encrust and contour over the substrate, occasionally with lumpy surfaces. Colonies' edges extend outward from substrate, are often undulated and generally rounded. May form in overlapping, shingle-like plates. With polyps retracted, corallite pits appear in honeycomb pattern. Brown or red-brown and gray; polyp centers white or green, edges lighter shade. Fragile.

**ABUNDANCE & DISTRIBUTION:** Occasional to uncommon Central American coast and offshore islands from Panama to Yucatan (see note).

**HABITAT & BEHAVIOR:** Inhabit sloping reef faces, attaching to and encrusting the rocky substrate; also reported to overgrow sponges.

**NOTE:** This species was first described in 1990; its distribution and abundance are not well documented. Some scientists consider this species a form of Mustard Hill Coral, *P. astreoides* [pg.121].

## BOULDER BRAIN CORAL
*Colpophyllia natans*
SUBORDER:
Faviida
FAMILY:
Faviidae

SIZE: Colony 1$^{1}/_{2}$ - 7 ft.
DEPTH: 2 - 175 ft.

**Colony with Closed-Valleys**

**Polyps Extended**
[far left]
**Polyps Retracted**
[near left]

## HONEYCOMB PLATE CORAL
*Porites colonensis*
SUBORDER:
Fungiida
FAMILY:
Poritidae

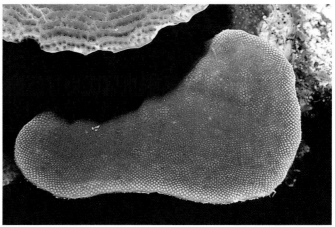

SIZE: Colony 6 - 18 in.
DEPTH: 10 - 90 ft.

*continued next page*

# Leaf, Plate & Sheet Corals

**Brown Variety**

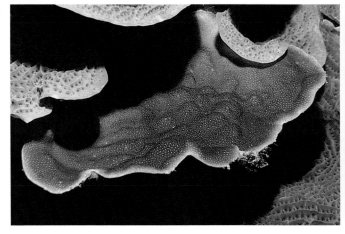

**VISUAL ID:** Colonies form saucers or plates with distinctive thin lines (septa) running toward the edges. Occasionally grow in overlapping shingle-like style. Ridges and valleys are not continuous. Corallite centers are distinctively nestled in rows against ridges' steep outer edges. Inner ridge faces slope more gently toward colonies' centers. Tan to yellow-brown, brown and gray; may fluoresce green, blue or purple tints. Fragile.

**ABUNDANCE & DISTRIBUTION:** Common to occasional South Florida, Bahamas, Caribbean.

**HABITAT & BEHAVIOR:** Inhabit sloping reef faces and along walls. Most common between 25-100 feet.

**NOTE:** Also commonly known as "Saucer Coral," "Sunray Plate Coral" and "Fragile Lettuce Coral." Formerly reported as *Helioseris cucullata*.

**Corallite Detail**

## HONEYCOMB PLATE CORAL
*continued from previous page*

**Detail: Honeycomb Corallite Pattern**

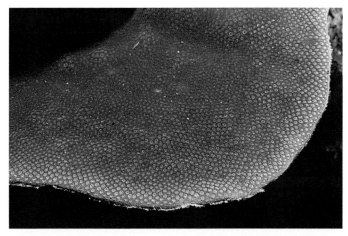

## SUNRAY LETTUCE CORAL
*Leptoseris cucullata*

SUBORDER:
Fungiida
FAMILY:
Agariciidae

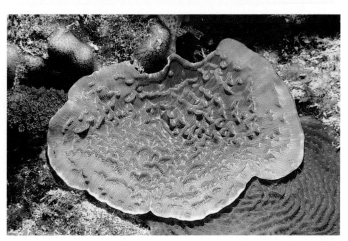

SIZE: Colony 4 - 10 in.
DEPTH: 10 - 280 ft.

**Overlapping, Shingle-like Pattern**

# Leaf, Plate & Sheet Corals

**VISUAL ID:** Colonies form small, thin saucer-like colonies. Ridges and long continuous valleys form an uneven pattern of concentric circles radiating from center of colony. The ridges of deep water colonies are often low and inconspicuous. Polyps are only present in the valleys of the upper surface; the underside is quite smooth. Shades of purplish brown, chocolate, yellow-brown, tan, and greenish tan. Fragile. Forma *contracta* colonies have pinched corallites and often grow in irregular, occasionally gnarled patterns.

**ABUNDANCE & DISTRIBUTION:** Occasional Florida, Bahamas, Caribbean.

**HABITAT & BEHAVIOR:** Inhabit sloping reef faces, under ledge overhangs and along walls.

**NOTE:** Visual identification of the two colonies on bottom of pages 136 &137 confirmed by collection and magnified examination.

**Low Profile Ridge Variety, Chocolate**

**Low Profile Ridge Variety, Yellow-brown**

*(USNM 92094)*

136

## FRAGILE SAUCER CORAL
*Agaricia fragilis*
SUBORDER:
Fungiida
FAMILY:
Agariciidae

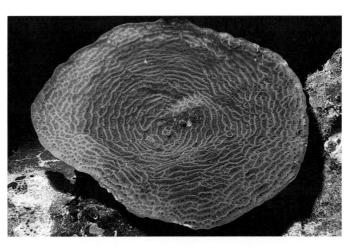

SIZE: Colony 4 - 6 in.
DEPTH: 20 - 180 ft.

**Yellow-brown Variety**

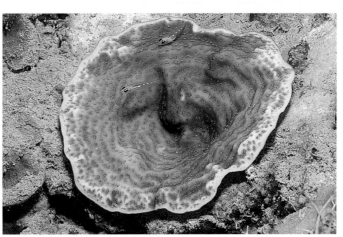

**Constricted Leaf Coral forma *contracta*:
Note Pinched Corallites**

*(USNM 91646)*

137

# Leaf, Plate & Sheet Corals

**VISUAL ID:** Colonies grow in massive, thin sheets or flattened plates that often form large whorls and occasionally spirals and bowls. Concentric rows of long rounded ridges and relatively wide valleys run parallel to the colonies' outer edges. Prominent, white star-like polyps in valleys' centers are distinctive of this species. Ridge ends are often tapered, rather than abruptly intersecting other ridges. Pencil-line thin septa, running between the polyp mouths, alternate in height and thickness (observation may require magnifying glass). Colonies' undersides have no polyps and are quite smooth. Yellow-brown to golden-brown and brown, may have greenish, bluish or grayish tints. Fragile.

**ABUNDANCE & DISTRIBUTION:** Common Caribbean.

**HABITAT & BEHAVIOR:** Inhabit sloping reef faces and along walls. One of the most abundant corals on deep reefs and walls. Most common between 65-120 feet. Massive overlapping plates often cover large areas.

**NOTE:** Also commonly known as "Lamarck's Lettuce-Leaf Coral."

**Detail:
Note distinctive
white star-like
polyps.**

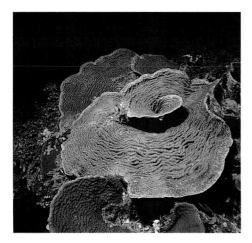

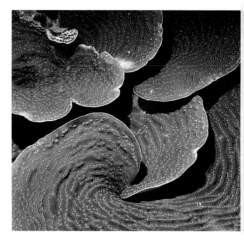

## LAMARCK'S SHEET CORAL
*Agaricia lamarcki*

SUBORDER:
Fungiida

FAMILY:
Agariciidae

SIZE: Colony 1-6 ft.
DEPTH: 15-150 ft.

## Growth Patterns
[left, right & bottom
both pages]

# Leaf, Plate & Sheet Corals

**VISUAL ID:** Colonies grow rounded, thin blades that commonly curve upward in the shape of fans or bowls often in a spiral design. Concentric rows of long, steep sloped ridges and relatively narrow, V-shaped valleys run parallel to the colonies' pale outer edges. Pale, dot-like polyps are centered in the valleys. Pencil-line thin septa running between polyp mouths are of equal size (observation may require magnifying glass). Colonies' undersides have no polyps and are quite smooth. Yellow-brown to golden-brown to brown, may have bluish, greenish or grayish tints. Fragile.

**ABUNDANCE & DISTRIBUTION:** Occasional Caribbean.

**HABITAT & BEHAVIOR:** Inhabit sloping reef faces and along walls. Most common between 75-150 feet.

**NOTE:** Also known as "Graham's Lettuce-leaf Coral."

**Bowl Shaped Colonies**

**VISUAL ID:** Colonies form rounded, thin blades that curve upward on flat or sloping substrate, growing in the shape of fans or bowls. On vertical walls large, spiral curving, overlapping plates may contour to the substrate. Occasionally grow in shingle-like fashion. Running around the upper surface are more-or-less continuous, wide, wavy valleys and ridges that parallel the outer edges. Corallite centers are distinctively nestled in rows against ridges' steep outer edges. Inner ridge faces slope more gently toward colonies' centers. The blades' undersides have no polyps and are quite smooth. Shades of brown to gray, often with yellowish, greenish or bluish tints; outer edge of blades often white. Fragile.

**ABUNDANCE & DISTRIBUTION:** Occasional Caribbean. Not reported Florida or Bahamas.

**HABITAT & BEHAVIOR:** Inhabit deep reefs, often on ledges or at the base of deep walls. Most common between 90-150 feet. Massive overlapping colonies occasionally cover large areas of the bottom.

### GRAHAM'S SHEET CORAL
*Agaricia grahamae*
SUBORDER:
Fungiida
FAMILY:
Agariciidae

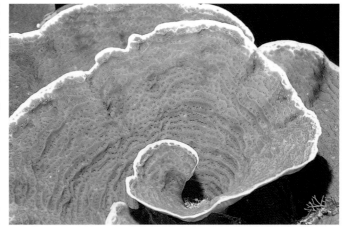

SIZE: Colony 1-6 ft.
DEPTH: 50-240 ft.

**Detail Comparison: Lamarck's Sheet Coral (left) note white star-like polyps and rounded ridges; Graham's Sheet Coral (right) note long parallel valleys with steep sloped ridges.**

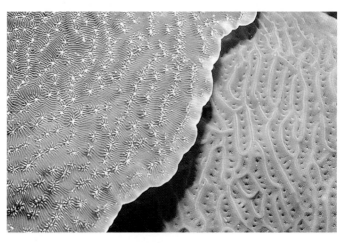

### SCROLL CORAL
*Agaricia undata*
SUBORDER:
Fungiina
FAMILY:
Agariciidae

SIZE: Colony 1 - 6 ft.
DEPTH: 50 - 250 ft.

*continued next page*

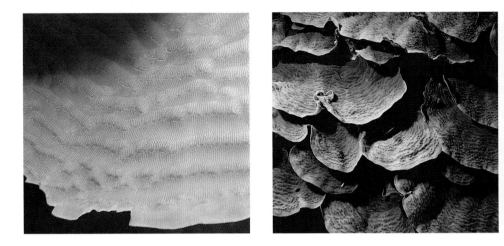

# VISUAL IDENTIFICATION KEY
# TO SIMILAR APPEARING PLATE & SHEET CORALS

Colonies of the following species often form structures with virtually identical shapes and sizes and often grow mixed together overlapping one another. Distinguishing the different species requires close observation of the valley and ridge structures, polyp placement and septa detail. The following guide should be helpful.

### NO RIDGES OR VALLEYS

BOULDER STAR CORAL, *Montastrea annularis*, morphotype (4) [pg.113]: small, prominently protruding, volcano-like corallites.

HONEYCOMB PLATE CORAL, *Porites colonensis* [pg.133]: porous, honeycomb-like corallites.

### RIDGES AND VALLEYS, CORALLITES CENTERED IN VALLEYS

LAMARCK'S SHEET CORAL, *Agaricia lamarcki* [pg.141]: thin, often whorled, plates. Prominent white, star-like polyps distinguish this species.

GRAHAM'S SHEET CORAL, *Agaricia grahamae* [pg.139]: thin, usually upturned plates forming fans and bowls with pale edges. Ridges raise sharply from V-shaped valleys.

PURPLE LETTUCE CORAL, *Agaricia agaricites* forma *purpurea* [pg. 145]: thick flat plates. Long parallel ridges and valleys mix with numerous short valleys and intersecting ridges. Ridges relatively tall and sharply raised.

### RIDGES AND VALLEYS, CORALLITES NESTLED AGAINST RIDGES' OUTER EDGE

SCROLL CORAL, *Agaricia undata* [pg.141]: ridges are long and continuous.

SUNRAY LETTUCE CORAL, *Leptoseris cucullata* [pg.135]: ridges tend to be short and discontinuous, septa more prominent than Scroll Coral [previous].

**SCROLL CORAL**
*continued from
previous page*

**Colony With Large
Overlapping Plates**

**Detail: Note Corallites
Nestled Against
Ridges' Outer Edge**
[far left]

**Shingle-like Colonies**
[near left]

**Mixture of Colonies
including: Lettuce,
Scroll and Lamarck's
Sheet Corals**

**Mixture of Colonies
including: Lettuce,
Sunray Lettuce,
Lamarck's Sheet and
Boulder Star Corals**

143

# Leaf, Plate & Sheet Corals

**VISUAL ID:** Colonies grow in four forms. Forma *agaricites* is thickly encrusting or hemispherical with ridges of different heights and discontinuous valleys in reticulated pattern. Forma *carinata* grows in thick ,flattened plates with prominent ridges and long valleys. Thick, bifacial, low, upright plates or ribbons extend from the surface. Forma *purpurea* grows in thick, flat plates and is distinguished by long continuous, parallel valleys with prominent ridges. Colonies may grow in shingle-like fashion. Forma *danai* grows a series of overlapping large, thick, bifacial, upright lobes. Tan to yellow-brown, grayish brown, brown and chocolate, can have bluish or purplish tints. Not especially fragile.

**ABUNDANCE & DISTRIBUTION:** Abundant to common Florida, Bahamas, Caribbean.

**HABITAT & BEHAVIOR:** Inhabit most marine environments from mangrove and back reef areas to outer reefs and walls. F. *agaricites* is the most common and generally inhabits shallow patch and back reef areas. The other forms are more common on fore reef slopes.

**Keeled Lettuce Coral**
**forma *carinata***
**Grows in Thick Plates**
**with Thick, Bifacial,**
**Upright Extensions**

**Purple Lettuce Coral**
**forma *purpurea***
**Grows in Flat Plates**
**with Long Continuous,**
**Parallel Valleys and**
**Tall Ridges**

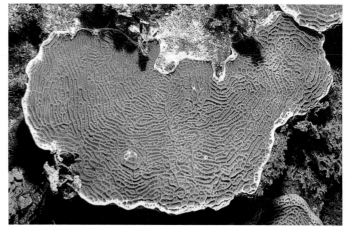

## LETTUCE CORAL
*Agaricia agaricites*
SUBORDER:
Fungiida
FAMILY:
Agariciidae

SIZE: Colony 4 in. - 3 ft.
DEPTH: 3 - 240 ft.

**Lettuce Coral
forma *agaricites*
Encrusts with
Discontinuous Valleys
and Ridges in
Reticulated Patterns**

**Scaled Lettuce Coral
forma *danai*
Grow in Series
of Thick, Bifacial,
Upright Lobes**

# Leaf, Plate & Sheet Corals

**VISUAL ID:** Colonies form small, generally circular, lumpy encrustations of densely packed corallites in reticulated patterns. Corallites have deep, often narrow or pinched pits. Long valleys or two-faced lobes are never present. Yellow-brown to brown or chocolate; frequently with white areas and blotches where zooxanthellae are absent.

**ABUNDANCE & DISTRIBUTION:** Occasional South Florida, Bahamas, Caribbean.

**HABITAT & BEHAVIOR:** Inhabit sloping reefs, undercut faces and canyon walls. Often in somewhat protected locations. Most common between 15-35 feet.

**NOTE:** This species is regarded by many scientists as a form of Lettuce Coral, *A. agaricites* forma *humilis* [previous]. Pictured specimen collected (USNM 91654) and visual identification confirmed by magnified examination.

---

**VISUAL ID:** Colonies form low clumps that resemble patches of leaf lettuce. The thin, upright blades have polyps on both sides. Wavy, parallel ridges run horizontally across the blade faces. Shades of brown to gray, often with yellowish, greenish or bluish tints. Blades fairly fragile.

**ABUNDANCE & DISTRIBUTION:** Abundant Northwest Caribbean, especially along Central American Coast; occasional to absent balance of Caribbean. Not reported Florida or Bahamas.

**HABITAT & BEHAVIOR:** Inhabit shallow reef tops, especially where wave action produces regular water movement. Numerous adjoining colonies can cover huge areas of reef tops. Most common between 15-30 feet. Narrow areas between blades provide shelter for numerous animals, including brittlestars, sea urchins and small eels. Watercress Alga [pg.205] often grows between the blades.

**Large Colonies can Cover Huge Areas**

## LOWRELIEF LETTUCE CORAL
*Agaricia humilis*
SUBORDER:
Fungiida
FAMILY:
Agariciidae

SIZE: Colony 3 - 5 in.
DEPTH: 5 - 80 ft.

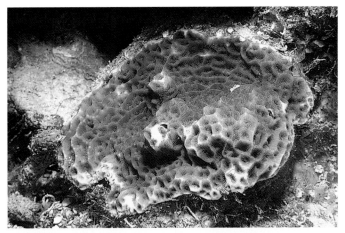

## THIN LEAF LETTUCE CORAL
*Agaricia tenuifolia*
SUBORDER:
Fungiida
FAMILY:
Agariciidae

SIZE: Colony 3 - 12 ft.
DEPTH: 6 - 90 ft.

### Blade Detail of Small Colony

# Fleshy Corals

**VISUAL ID:** Colonies form flat plates, mounds and hemispherical domes. Ridges border the plates and run toward, and occasionally across, the colonies' centers. Ridges may intertwine and there are often independent ridges and knobs. (Similar Ridged Cactus Coral [next] ridges do not reach colonies' centers or intertwine.) Valleys relatively deep and somewhat narrow compared to those of Ridged Cactus Coral. Ridges and valleys are usually of contrasting colors or shades. Color variable, commonly in shades of green, brown or gray. Colonies and especially their ridges may appear fleshy.

**ABUNDANCE & DISTRIBUTION:** Occasional South Florida, Bahamas, Caribbean.

**HABITAT & BEHAVIOR:** Tend to inhabit shaded areas of shallow to moderately deep reefs. Most common between 25-75 feet. Polyps retracted during day.

**NOTE:** Some scientists believe this species is a growth form of Ridged Cactus Coral [next]. Also commonly known as "Fat Fungus Coral."

**Plate-like
Growth Pattern**

**Polyps Extended
at Night:
Note Tentacles
Along Ridges' Edges**

### LOWRIDGE CACTUS CORAL

*Mycetophyllia danaana*

SUBORDER:
Faviida
FAMILY:
Mussidae

SIZE: Colony 6 - 15 in.
DEPTH: 10 - 100 ft.

**Hemispherical Dome Growth Pattern**

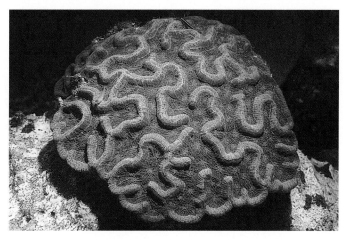

**Young Colony**

# Fleshy Corals

**VISUAL ID:** Colonies form flat, scalloped-edged plates. Ridges border the plates and run toward colonies' centers. Ridges do not extend to center, join or intertwine; there are no independent ridges (compare similar Lowridge Cactus Coral [previous]). Valleys generally wide and relatively shallow. Colonies, and especially their ridges, may appear fleshy. Ridges and valleys are usually of contrasting colors or shades. Color variable; commonly in shades of green, brown or gray.

**ABUNDANCE & DISTRIBUTION:** Occasional South Florida, Bahamas, Caribbean.

**HABITAT & BEHAVIOR:** Tend to inhabit shaded areas of moderate and deeper reefs, often on ledges and along walls. Most common between 40-100 feet. Polyps retracted during day.

**NOTE:** Also commonly known as "Large Cactus Coral" and "Fungus Coral."

### Brown & Gray Variety

**VISUAL ID:** Colonies usually grow in thin, flat or somewhat convex, generally circular plates, but occasionally form mounds and domes. Large, raised star-shaped corallites are distinctive. Ridges border the plates and may run toward the colonies' centers, especially in the shallower waters of their depth range. On occasion there may also be short independent ridges. In deeper water the ridges become less pronounced and occasionally disappear altogether. Ridges and corallites are often of light colors, contrasting with darker valleys in shades of green, brown or gray.

**ABUNDANCE & DISTRIBUTION:** Occasional South Florida, Bahamas, Caribbean.

**HABITAT & BEHAVIOR:** Inhabit most moderate to deep reef environments, from patch reefs to steep slopes and wall drop-offs. Most common between 65-130 feet. Polyps retracted during the day.

**NOTE:** Also commonly known as "Thin Fungus Coral."

## RIDGED CACTUS CORAL
*Mycetophyllia*
*lamarckiana*
SUBORDER:
Faviida
FAMILY:
Mussidae

SIZE: Colony 6 - 12 in.
DEPTH: 10 - 190 ft.

**Dying Colony
Showing Skeleton**

## KNOBBY CACTUS CORAL
*Mycetophyllia aliciae*
SUBORDER:
Faviida
FAMILY:
Mussidae

SIZE: Colony 6 - 18 in.
DEPTH: 50 - 240 ft.

*continued next page*

# Fleshy Corals

**Deep Water Growth Pattern without Ridges**

**VISUAL ID:** Colonies form thin, flattened, often semicircular plates, and occasionally irregular mounds that encrust the substrate. Ridges border the plates and run toward the colonies' centers forming narrow valleys; occasionally there are a few independent ridges. Only member of genus where ridges often join to form closed valleys. Valleys shallow with central, single row of small, knob-like corallites. Ridges are low, flattened and have a thin groove along top. Ridges and corallites are usually of light color, contrasting with darker valleys in shades of green, red-brown, brown or gray.

**ABUNDANCE & DISTRIBUTION:** Occasional South Florida, Bahamas, Caribbean.

**HABITAT & BEHAVIOR:** Tend to inhabit shaded areas of midrange reefs and along walls. Most common between 30-70 feet. Polyps retracted during day.

**NOTE:** Also commonly known as "Grooved Fungus Coral."

**Detail: Note Groove in Ridges and Knob-Like Corallites**

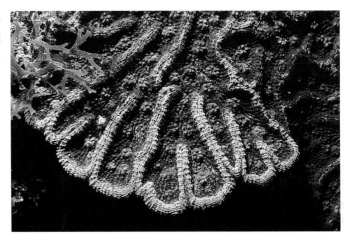

### KNOBBY CACTUS CORAL
*continued from previous page*
**Young Colony**

### ROUGH CACTUS CORAL
*Mycetophyllia ferox*
SUBORDER:
Faviida
FAMILY:
Mussidae

SIZE: Colony 1-2 ft.
DEPTH: 25-120 ft.

**Colony Encrusting Reef Top**

153

# Fleshy Corals

**VISUAL ID:** Colonies form thin, usually circular plates that generally conform to the contours of the substrate. Only member of genus without ridges. Surface covered with rounded bumps (polyps located at center). Shades of green, brown, gray, blue-gray and may have iridescent tints. Only Caribbean species of coral whose polyps lack tentacles.

**ABUNDANCE & DISTRIBUTION:** Occasional Caribbean. Not reported South Florida or Bahamas.

**HABITAT & BEHAVIOR:** Inhabit shaded areas of deep reefs; most common along walls. Polyps retracted during day.

---

**VISUAL ID:** Colonies form small, oval to hemispherical domes. Highly convoluted with fleshy ridges and deep, narrow, often closed valleys. (Small colonies of similar Lowridge Cactus Coral [pg.149] distinguished by wide, open valleys.) Colors quite variable, including shades of yellow, green, brown and gray. Occasionally iridescent tints of orange or blue. Ridges and valleys usually of contrasting shades or colors. Light colored, thin line along ridge tops.

**ABUNDANCE & DISTRIBUTION:** Populations highly variable from locality to locality; abundant to rare South Florida, Bahamas, Caribbean.

**HABITAT & BEHAVIOR:** Inhabit a wide range of shallow water environments, including fringing reefs, back reefs, patch reefs and areas of high sedimentation. Most common between 3-30 feet. Polyps retracted during day.

**NOTE:** Common name comes from sharp skeletal spines which are hidden under the fleshy tissue. Also commonly known as "Cactus Coral," "Fleshy Cactus Coral" and "Stalked Cactus Coral."

---

**VISUAL ID:** Colonies form small ova,l to hemispherical domes. Fleshy ridges with rough, irregular polygonal valleys. Valleys usually contain only one or two polyps. Light colored, thin line along ridgetops. Ridges commonly brown, occasionally green, pinkish or even purple; valleys pale to white.

**ABUNDANCE & DISTRIBUTION:** Common to occasional South Florida, Bahamas, Florida.

**HABITAT & BEHAVIOR:** Inhabit a wide range of shallow water environments, including fringing reefs, back reefs, patch reefs and areas of high sedimentation. Most common between 10-35 feet. Polyps retracted during day.

**NOTE:** Also commonly known as "Polygonal Coral."

### RIDGELESS CACTUS CORAL
*Mycetophyllia reesi*
SUBORDER:
Faviida
FAMILY:
Mussidae

SIZE: Colony 1 - 2 ft.
DEPTH: 60 - 220 ft.

### SINUOUS CACTUS CORAL
*Isophyllia sinuosa*
SUBORDER:
Faviida
FAMILY:
Mussidae

SIZE: Colony 2¹/₂ - 8 in.
DEPTH: 3 - 85 ft.

### ROUGH STAR CORAL
*Isophyllastrea rigida*
SUBORDER:
Faviida
FAMILY:
Mussidae

SIZE: Colony 3 - 7 in.
DEPTH: 3 - 65 ft.

# Fleshy Corals

**VISUAL ID:** Single, large, fleshy, circular to oval polyp. Underlying skeleton often evident in the form of raised radiating lines. Central area of corallite usually flat to somewhat convex, rarely concave. Darker shades of gray to brown, green, and blue-green; base color often radially streaked with lighter shade. May fluoresce. Positive identification of this and the next two species requires magnified examination (see next description). There are no visual clues distinguishing Solitary Disk Coral [next]; Atlantic Mushroom Coral [next page] usually has a rougher texture and lighter colors.

**ABUNDANCE & DISTRIBUTION:** Occasional South Florida, Bahamas, Caribbean.

**HABITAT & BEHAVIOR:** Generally inhabit deep reefs and walls, occasionally shallower. Prefer shaded areas on rocky substrates and also grow in low-light conditions under ledge overhangs and in cave openings. Polyp tentacles retracted during day.

**NOTE:** Visual identification of pictured specimens was verified by collection and magnified examination of septa. Also commonly known as "Solitary Disk Coral" and "Smooth Disk Coral."

**Juveniles, Such as Pictured Specimen, Cannot be Positively Identified**

**VISUAL ID:** Single, large, fleshy, circular to oval polyp. Underlying skeleton often evident in the form of raised radiating lines. Central area of corallite usually flat to somewhat concave, rarely convex. Darker shades of gray to brown, green, and blue-green; base color often radially streaked with lighter shade. May fluoresce. Smallest of the three disk coral species. Positive identification requires magnified examination of erect projections growing from the septa, called teeth. This species has rough, irregular, thin cylindrical teeth; Artichoke Coral [previous] has spike or pick-shaped teeth; and Atlantic Mushroom [next] has large, triangular teeth.

**ABUNDANCE & DISTRIBUTION:** Occasional South Florida, Bahamas, Caribbean.

**HABITAT & BEHAVIOR:** Generally inhabit deep reefs and walls, occasionally shallower. Prefer shaded areas on rocky substrates and also grow in low-light conditions under ledge overhangs and in cave openings. Polyp tentacles retracted during day.

**NOTE:** Visual identification of pictured specimens was verified by collection (USNM 91560) and magnified examination of septa.

## ARTICHOKE CORAL
*Scolymia cubensis*
SUBORDER:
Faviida
FAMILY:
Mussidae

SIZE: Polyp 1½ - 4 in.
DEPTH: 30 - 260 ft.

### Color Variety

*(USNM 91664)*

## SOLITARY DISK CORAL
*Scolymia wellsi*
SUBORDER:
Faviida
FAMILY:
Mussidae

SIZE: Polyp 1 - 2 ¾ in.
DEPTH: 30 - 260 ft.

*continued next page*

# Fleshy Corals

Color Variety

*(USNM 91665)*

**VISUAL ID:** Single, large, fleshy, circular to oval polyp with rough, warty texture. Central area of corallite usually concave to flat, rarely convex. Lighter shades of gray to green, blue-green and brown. (Generally texture rougher and color shades lighter than two previous species.) Caribbean's largest solitary polyp coral. Size alone can confirm identification if over four inches. If less, positive identification requires magnified examination of corallite structure (see previous description).

**ABUNDANCE & DISTRIBUTION:** Occasional South Florida, Bahamas, Caribbean.

**HABITAT & BEHAVIOR:** Inhabit deep reef environments and walls. Most common between 60-100 feet. Prefer well-lighted areas on rocky substrates and outcroppings. Polyp tentacles retracted during day.

**NOTE:** Visual identification of pictured specimens was verified by magnified examination of triangular septal teeth. D.P. Fenner concludes that this is not a separate species, but a form of Spiny Flower Coral [next], *Bull. Mar. Sci.*, in press 1992.

## SOLITARY DISK CORAL
*continued from previous page*
### Color Variety

*(USNM 91661)*

## ATLANTIC MUSHROOM CORAL
*Scolymia lacera*
SUBORDER:
Faviida
FAMILY:
Mussidae

SIZE: Polyp 2 $\frac{1}{2}$ - 6 in.
DEPTH: 30 - 260 ft.

### Color Varieties

*(USNM 91661)*

# Fleshy Corals – Cup & Flower Corals

**VISUAL ID:** Colonies formed of large fleshy polyps with rough, blemished texture. Although the polyps are well-separated on the tips of a branched structure, their expanded fleshy tissues press against adjacent individuals so tightly that an overall colony appears as a solid mound. The polyp's skeleton, composed of numerous sharp spiked plates (septa) [below right], is the source of the common name. Shades of gray, may have tints of green, blue and even fluorescent reddish orange or pink (fluorescent color disappears if hand light or strobe is used).

**ABUNDANCE & DISTRIBUTION:** Common to occasional South Florida, Bahamas, Caribbean.

**HABITAT & BEHAVIOR:** Inhabit most reef environments. Most common between 20-80 feet. Polyps extend tentacles only at night.

**NOTE:** Also commonly known as "Large Flower Coral."

**Polyp Tentacles Extended at Night**

**VISUAL ID:** Colonial polyps, often in small clusters. Corallites cone-shaped with circular to elliptical rims and deep central pits. Tall, thin, rounded, protruding septa radiate from the pit and extend around the rim lip. Often lavender or white, occasionally pink or pale green. Fragile. Ahermatypic.

**ABUNDANCE & DISTRIBUTION:** Occasional Caribbean. Not reported Florida or Bahamas.

**HABITAT & BEHAVIOR:** Inhabit the ceilings of caves, under ledge overhangs usually where there is some water circulation. Most common below 80 feet.

**NOTE:** Visual identification of pictured specimens confirmed by collection (USNM 92084) and magnified examination.

## SPINY FLOWER CORAL
*Mussa angulosa*
SUBORDER:
Faviida
FAMILY:
Mussidae

SIZE: Colony ¹/₂ - 2 ft.
Polyp 1¹/₂ - 4 in.
DEPTH: 5 - 180 ft.

**Comparison of Living and Dead Polyp: Note Triangular Septal Teeth**

## BAROQUE CAVE CORAL
*Thalamophyllia riisei*
SUBORDER:
Caryophylliida
FAMILY:
Caryophylliidae

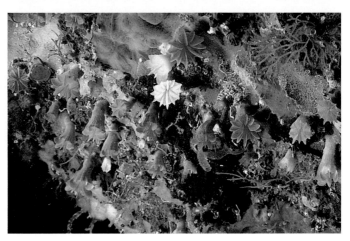

SIZE: Polyp ¹/₄ - ¹/₂ in.
DEPTH: 50 - 1,000 ft.

# Cup & Flower Corals

**VISUAL ID:** Clumps of widely spaced polyps on long stalks, that appear to originate from a central core, form hemispherical mounds. Corallites round to oval. Shades of yellow-brown to brown and gray, often with blue to blue-green to green tinting that may be somewhat iridescent. A rare variant, forma *flabellata*, is distinguished by extremely long (up to six inches), narrow (about one-half inch) corallites.

**ABUNDANCE & DISTRIBUTION:** Common to occasional South Florida, Bahamas Caribbean.

**HABITAT & BEHAVIOR:** Inhabit most reef environments, prefer somewhat shaded protected areas. Most common between 15-90 feet. Occasionally multiple colonies cover large area of the reef. Extend tentacles at night.

**Extended Polyp Detail**

**Corallite Detail, Typical Form**

### SMOOTH FLOWER CORAL
*Eusmilia fastigiata*
SUBORDER:
Caryophylliida
FAMILY:
Caryophylliidae

SIZE: Colony $\frac{1}{2}$- 2 $\frac{1}{2}$ ft.
Polyps $\frac{3}{4}$-1$\frac{1}{4}$ in.
DEPTH: 3-200 ft.

**Colony with Polyps
Extended at Night**

**Elongate Smooth
Flower Coral
forma *flabellata*,
Corallite Detail**

# Cup & Flower Corals

**VISUAL ID:** Brilliant red to orange or yellow polyp clumps that often form hemispherical mounds. Tissue covering skeleton usually deeper red to orange, while tentacles often bright orange to yellow. Colonies may contain only a few or hundreds of polyps. Ahermatypic.

**ABUNDANCE & DISTRIBUTION:** Scattered distribution throughout Bahamas, eastern and southern Caribbean. May be abundant in localized areas, while absent in similar environments around same island. Absent or rare northwest Caribbean and Florida.

**HABITAT & BEHAVIOR:** Prefer shaded areas in a wide range of environments, from pilings under docks, to caves in shallow reefs, to undercut faces and walls on deeper reefs. A clear water species that prefers some water movement. A few polyps may be extended during day, but full extension of entire colony normally occurs only at night.

**NOTE:** Also commonly known as "Orange Tube Coral," "Orange Flower Coral" and "Red or Orange Coral."

**VISUAL ID:** Small, solitary polyp. Corallite cone-shaped with base re-expanding to encrust and attach to hard substrate (occasionally free when base attaches to and envelops a small pebble). Rim (calice) of corallite oval to elliptical. Twelve large septa of equal size can be seen by unaided eye, with several smaller septa between. Small septal ridges continue down sides of corallite resulting in a corrugated texture. Red to pink, orange, light brown and white. Ahermatypic.

**ABUNDANCE & DISTRIBUTION:** Uncommon (within safe diving limits) Florida, Bahamas, Caribbean.

**HABITAT & BEHAVIOR:** Inhabit areas with hard substrates or gravel. Bases may be covered with sand or gravel exposing only the rims of corallites. Tend to inhabit shallower waters off Florida's northern coasts.

**NOTE:** Pictured specimen collected (USNM 92271) at 80 feet, off Jacksonville, Florida; identification confirmed by magnified examination.

## ORANGE CUP CORAL
*Tubastraea coccinea*
SUBORDER:
Dendrophylliina
FAMILY:
Dendrophylliidae

SIZE: Colony 3-12 in.
Polyp $1/2$ -$3/4$ in.
DEPTH: 3-120 ft.

**Hemispherical Colony**

**Colonies on
Undercut Reef Face**
[far left]

**Colonies on
Dock Piling at Night**
[near left]

## POROUS CUP CORAL
*Balanophyllia floridana*
SUBORDER:
Dendrophylliina
FAMILY:
Dendrophylliidae

SIZE: Diameter $1/2$ - 1 in.
Height $3/4$ - $1^1/2$ in.
DEPTH: 80 - 600 ft.

# Cup & Flower Corals

**VISUAL ID:** Small, solitary polyps. Slightly tapering, cylindrical corallite with flared rim and base re-expanding to encrust and attach to hard substrate. Rim (calice) of corallite circular to slightly oval. Six, tall primary septa, and six smaller secondary septa can be seen by unaided eye. Septal ridges down sides of corallite not apparent to unaided eye. Pale to bright pink. Ahermatypic.

**ABUNDANCE & DISTRIBUTION:** Rare, Roatan, Honduras; additional distribution unknown (see note).

**HABITAT & BEHAVIOR:** Inhabit dark recesses such as cave ceilings and under ledge overhangs. Other habitats unknown (see note).

**NOTE:** Pictured specimen collected (USNM 92087) at 15 feet, off Roatan, Honduras. Magnified examination determined this to be one of several scientifically undescribed shallow water species in the Caribbean.

---

**VISUAL ID:** Colonial; corallites may be clustered in small groups or appear to be solitary. Solitary examples are joined to nearby corallites by encrusting bases that may be hidden from view by overgrowing organisms. Corallites are slightly tapering and cylindrical with flared rims (calice). Six, tall, thick primary septa, and six smaller secondary septa can be seen by unaided eye. Fine septal ridges continue down sides of corallites resulting in a subtle corrugated texture, although not always obvious to the unaided eye. Bright orange to pink. Ahermatypic.

**ABUNDANCE & DISTRIBUTION:** Occasional Caribbean, Bahamas and Gulf of Mexico.

**HABITAT & BEHAVIOR:** Inhabit dark recesses such as cave ceilings and under ledge overhangs.

**NOTE:** Identification of pictured specimans confirmed by collection and magnified examination: right (USNM 91651) at 15 feet, Roatan, Honduras; below ( USNM 91655) at 65 t, Conception Island, Bahamas; below right (USNM 91659) at 85 feet, San Salvador, Bahamas.

**Note Corrugated Texture of Corallite's Sides**

166

## PINK SOLITARY CORAL
*Balanophyllia n. sp.*
**SUBORDER:**
Dendrophylliina
**FAMILY:**
Dendrophylliidae

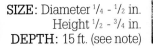

**SIZE:** Diameter ¹/₄ - ¹/₂ in.
Height ¹/₂ - ³/₄ in.
**DEPTH:** 15 ft. (see note)

## ORANGE SOLITARY CORAL
*Rhizopsammia goesi*
**SUBORDER:**
Dendrophylliina
**FAMILY:**
Dendrophylliidae

**SIZE:** Diameter ¹/₄ - ¹/₂ in.
Height ¹/₄ - ¹/₂ in.
**DEPTH:** 15-385 ft.

**Solitary Appearing Corallites are Joined By Encrusting Bases**

# Cup & Flower Corals

**VISUAL ID:** Colonies form a thin encrusting base from which corallites protrude. Often the corallites appear unconnected because of overgrowing sponge, algae and other organisms, but the connection between two or three individuals is usually obvious. Corallites are circular to elliptical with tall, thin, rounded, protruding septa around the rims and deep central pits. There are usually twelve obvious, large septa of nearly equal size, and numerous smaller ones depending on corallite size. (Similar Lesser Speckled Cup Coral [next] has only six large septa.) Orange-brown, brown, pink and lavender; central pit often pale green. Brown speckled pigmentation is distinctive of this species. Occasionally large individual polyps do not show this pigmentation. Ahermatypic.

**ABUNDANCE & DISTRIBUTION:** Common Caribbean; occasional Florida, Bahamas.

**HABITAT & BEHAVIOR:** Inhabit the ceilings of caves, under ledge overhangs, and occasionally on the underside of deep sheet and plate corals.

*(USNM 91652)*                                        *(USNM 92081)*

**VISUAL ID:** Colonies form small encrusting groups of polyps. Often the corallites appear unconnected because of overgrowing sponge, algae and other organisms. Corallites are circular to elliptical with deep central pits. Six tall, thin, rounded septa protrude noticeably around the rim. (Similar Speckled Cup Coral [previous] distinguished by twelve large septa of nearly equal size.) Numerous smaller septa are usually apparent. Light green, orange-brown, brown, pink, lavender and white. May have some brown speckled pigmentation. Center (mouth area of polyp) often of lighter and/or different color. Ahermatypic.

**ABUNDANCE & DISTRIBUTION:** Occasional Florida, Bahamas, Caribbean.

**HABITAT & BEHAVIOR:** Attach to and encrust the underside of rocks, ledge overhangs and cave ceilings. Often only the top of the polyp is visible because the body is hidden by encrusting sponge, algae or other growths.

**NOTE:** Pictured specimens collected (USNM 91658) and visual identification confirmed by magnified examination.

### SPECKLED CUP CORAL
*Rhizosmilia maculata*
SUBORDER:
Caryophylliida
FAMILY:
Caryophylliidae

SIZE: Corallite ¹/₄ - ¹/₂ in.,
max. 1 in.
DEPTH: 10 - 500 ft.

**Brown Variety with
Green Centers:
Note Dark Brown
Speckles**

**Large Single Polyps**
[left]

### LESSER SPECKLED CUP CORAL
*Colangia immersa*
SUBORDER:
Faviida
FAMILY:
Rhizangiidae

SIZE: Polyp ¹/₂ in.
DEPTH: 10 - 300 ft.

*continued next page*

# Cup & Flower Corals

**Lavender Variety, Encrusting Underside of Ledge Overhang**

*(USNM 92091)*

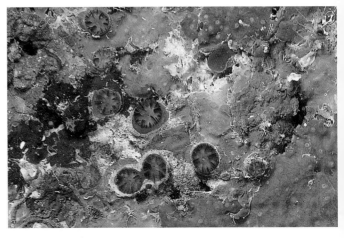

**VISUAL ID:** Colonies form small encrusting groups of polyps. Often the corallites appear unconnected because of overgrowing sponge, algae and other organisms. Corallites are tall and cylindrical with sharp, prickly protrusions and deep central pits. Six tall, thin, rounded septa and six, somewhat smaller, secondary septa protrude noticeably around the circular rims. Smaller septa are usually apparent. Light brown. Ahermatypic.

**ABUNDANCE & DISTRIBUTION:** Rare, Roatan, Honduras: additional distribution unknown (see note).

**HABITAT & BEHAVIOR:** Inhabit dark, deep recesses of cave ceilings. Other habitats unknown (see note). Often only the top of the polyp is visible because the body is hidden by encrusting sponge, algae or other growths.

**NOTE:** Pictured specimen collected at 35 feet, off Roatan, Honduras. Magnified examination determined this to be one of several scientifically undescribed shallow water species in the Caribbean

**VISUAL ID:** Colonies form small encrusting groups of polyps. Corallites circular with deep central pits. Six protruding primary and six, somewhat smaller, secondary septa around rims. Brown color, ranging from yellow-brown to brown to red-brown is distinctive of this species. Never speckled like similar Speckled Cup Coral [previous page]. Ahermatypic.

**ABUNDANCE & DISTRIBUTION:** Occasional Florida, Bahamas, Caribbean.

**HABITAT & BEHAVIOR:** Attach to and encrust the underside of rocks, ledge overhangs and cave ceilings. Often only the top of the polyp is visible because the body is hidden by encrusting sponge, algae or other growths. Most common between 1-60 feet.

## LESSER SPECKLED CUP CORAL
*continued from previous page*

**Encrusting Ceiling of Shallow Tidal Cave**

*(USNM 92086)*

## CRYPTIC CAVE CORAL
*Colangia n. sp.*
SUBORDER:
Faviina
FAMILY:
Rhizangiidae

SIZE: Polyp $1/4$ in.
DEPTH: 35 ft. (see note)

## HIDDEN CUP CORAL
*Phyllangia americana*
SUBORDER:
Faviina
FAMILY:
Rhizangiidae

SIZE: Polyp $1/2$ in.
DEPTH: 1 - 100 ft.

*continued next page*

**171**

# Cup & Flower Corals

**VISUAL ID:** Colonies appear as scattered groups of tiny individual polyps; however, corallite bases are joined by thin, often obscured encrustations. Corallites cylindrical; septa often appear as rows of whitish dots radiating from centers and wrapping around rims. Shades of red-brown to brown. Ahermatypic.

**ABUNDANCE & DISTRIBUTION:** Occasional Florida, Bahamas, Caribbean.

**HABITAT & BEHAVIOR:** Attach to and encrust the underside of rocks, coral rubble, ledge overhangs and cave ceilings. Often only the tip of the polyp is visible because the body is hidden by encrusting sponge, algae or other growths. Most common between 1-20 feet.

**NOTE:** Visual identification of pictured specimens confirmed by collection (USNM 92090) and magnified examination.

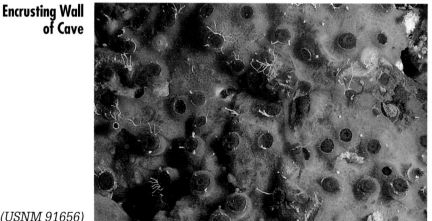

*(USNM 91656)*

## HIDDEN CUP CORAL
*continued from
previous page*
**Yellow-brown Variety**

*(USNM 92086)*

## DWARF CUP CORAL
*Astrangia solitaria*
SUBORDER:
Faviida
FAMILY:
Rhizangiidae

SIZE: Polyp diameter
$\frac{1}{8}$ - $\frac{1}{4}$ in.
height $\frac{1}{8}$ - $\frac{3}{4}$ in.
DEPTH: 1 - 135 ft.

**Polyps Expanded**

*(USNM 91657)*

# Cup & Flower Corals

**VISUAL ID:** Colonies form clusters of circular to oval corallites with common encrusting base. Numerous, tall rounded septa and separated inner ends (pali) in central pit visible to unaided eye. Colonies expand by asexual budding from the edges of common base. Septa red-brown; pali and central pit white. Ahermatypic.

**ABUNDANCE & DISTRIBUTION:** Uncommon Bahamas, Caribbean, Gulf of Mexico.

**HABITAT & BEHAVIOR:** Attach to and encrust the underside ledge overhangs and cave ceilings.

**NOTE:** Pictured specimen collected (USNM 92280) at 125 feet, off West Caicos, Turks & Caicos Islands and visual identification confirmed by magnified examination.

---

**VISUAL ID:** Colonies formed of circular corallites with common encrusting base. Six to twelve high rounded septa, with several smaller septa between and numerous lobes in central pit visible to unaided eye. Colonies expand by asexual budding from the edges of common base. Shades of white, occasionally tinted with pink. Ahermatypic.

**ABUNDANCE & DISTRIBUTION:** Rare off West Palm Beach. Additional distribution unknown (See note).

**HABITAT & BEHAVIOR:** Attach to and encrust the underside ledge overhangs and cave ceilings.

**NOTE:** Pictured specimen collected (USNM 92080) at 70 feet, off West Palm Beach, Florida. Magnified examination determined this to be one of several scientifically undescribed shallow water species and the first time this genus has been reported in the West Atlantic.

---

**VISUAL ID:** Solitary, cylindrical, circular to slightly elliptical corallites with twelve large, rounded septa, and three smaller septa between visible to unaided eye. Separated inner ends of septa (pali) form a light colored elliptical ring around deep central pit. Upper half of corallite shades of brown; basal deposits creamy white. Ahermatypic.

**ABUNDANCE & DISTRIBUTION:** Uncommon Bahamas, Caribbean. Not reported Florida.

**HABITAT & BEHAVIOR:** Firmly attach to hard substrate on the underside of ledge overhangs and cave ceilings. Occasionally in the recesses of small cavities.

**NOTE:** Pictured specimen collected (USNM 91667) at 70 feet, off San Salvador, Bahamas. Magnified examination determined this to be one of several known, but scientifically undescribed shallow water species.

### TWOTONE CUP CORAL
*Phacelocyathus flos*
**SUBORDER:**
Caryophylliida
**FAMILY:**
Caryophylliidae

**SIZE:** Polyp diameter
$^1/_4$ - $^1/_2$ in.
**DEPTH:** 70 - 1,700 ft.

### ORNATE CUP CORAL
*Coenocyathus n. sp.*
**SUBORDER:**
Caryophylliida
**FAMILY:**
Caryophylliidae

**SIZE:** Polyp diameter
$^1/_8$ - $^1/_4$ in.
**DEPTH:** 70 ft. (see note)

### BUTTON CUP CORAL
*Caryophyllia n. sp.*
**SUBORDER:**
Caryophylliida
**FAMILY:**
Caryophylliidae

**SIZE:** Polyp diameter
$^1/_8$ - $^1/_4$ in.
**DEPTH:** 50 - 550 ft.

# Class Anthozoa
# Subclass Ceriantipatharia
# Order Antipatharia

(An-tih-path-AIR-ee-ah/Gr. against disease)

## BLACK CORALS

Black corals are generally thought to be deep dwellers, but about half of the approximately 30 species in the Caribbean area can be found within safe scuba diving depths and several grow in surprisingly shallow water. Black coral polyps secrete a protein material, usually black in color, that becomes extremely hard and strong by a tanning process. This material is laid down in **concentric layers** forming branched or wire-like structures (skeleton). When a branch is crosscut these layers resemble the growth rings of a tree. The branching pattern of many species is unique and often the key to visual identification. Several species have tiny branchlets called **pinnules**.

Black coral polyps do not form corallite "homes" like stony corals, but instead simply live on the skeletal surface. Each polyp has six, small, non-retractable **tentacles** that can, however, expand or contract to some degree. The tentacles are normally visible to the unaided eye and are an important key in recognizing a colonial structure as black coral. The individual polyps of many species are recognizable because they are spaced apart from one another and their clusters of tentacles resemble barbs of barbed wire. Polyps of other species are spaced close so together that they are difficult to distinguish and appear as a mass of inseparable tentacles.

The polyp tissue of most black corals is somewhat translucent and color pigments only tint the colony gray, brown, rust-red, or green. Occasionally the pigments may be intense and dramatic, especially wire corals which are bright yellow-green or red.

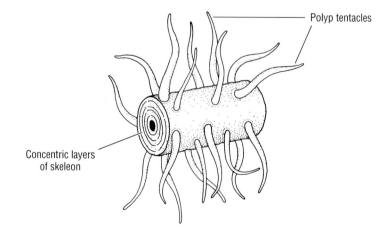

Polyp tentacles

Concentric layers
of skeleon

A few black coral species attain considerable size and their branches are collected, cut, fashioned, polished and sold by jewelers as a semiprecious material. The value of these trinkets comes more from jewelers' propaganda of rareness and the danger associated with deep diving to collect branches, than from any innate property of the material itself. In fact, the black coral species most frequently used by jewelers is neither rare or found particularly deep — on occasion a snorkeler might even sight a colony! Unfortunately, it is now rare in many areas from overharvesting. The great black coral forests of Grand Cayman and Cozumel are only a memory. It will take these slow growing colonies over 100 years to reestablish themselves.

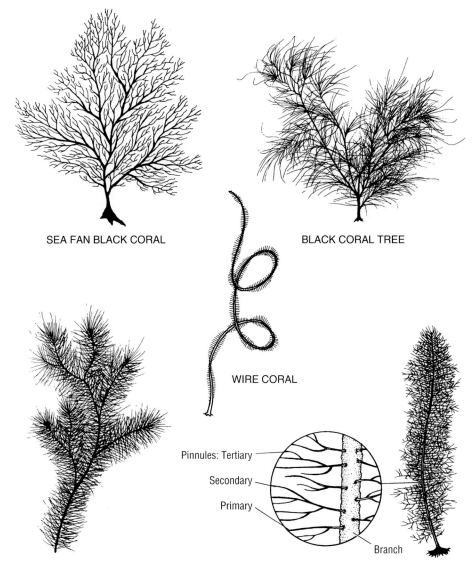

SEA FAN BLACK CORAL

BLACK CORAL TREE

WIRE CORAL

Pinnules: Tertiary

Secondary

Primary

Branch

BOTTLE-BRUSH BUSH BLACK CORAL

BOTTLE BRUSH BLACK CORAL

Black Corals

**VISUAL ID:** Bushy, branched colonies of primary stalks, with long, thin, scraggly branchlets. Primary branches golden-brown to brown to black and may be tinted red, green or blue. Branchlets are often of lighter color. It is now rare to see colonies over four feet in height because of overharvesting (see note).

**ABUNDANCE & DISTRIBUTION:** Common to uncommon Bahamas, Caribbean; rare South Florida. Because of overharvesting, now rare in many locations.

**HABITAT & BEHAVIOR:** In shallow water, occasionally inhabit caves and under large overhangs. In deep water, primarily inhabit canyons and wall faces with some current or periodic water movement. Most common between 80 and 240 feet; in many locations rarely found above 150 feet because of over harvesting.

**NOTE:** This species, prized by the jewelry industry, is often called "Kings Coral." Although these colonies are well known they have yet to be scientifically described.

**SIMILAR SPECIES:** *A. salix* often confused with this species is common between 300-1000 feet.

*(USNM 92276)*

**VISUAL ID:** Profuse primary and secondary branches extend from a holdfast in nearly a single plane. Thin, pinnate branchlets line either side of the secondary branches, resembling large feathers. Primary and secondary branches golden-brown to brown, gray and black; may be tinted red, green or blue. Branchlets are often of lighter color.

**ABUNDANCE & DISTRIBUTION:** Common to uncommon Bahamas, Caribbean; rare South Florida.

**HABITAT & BEHAVIOR:** In shallow water, inhabit caves and under large overhangs. In deep water, inhabit most reef environments including reef slopes, and along walls. Most common between 60 and 180 feet. Often in old deep shipwrecks. A few species of small stalked barnacles [See *Reef Creature Identification*, pg. 185] and other invertebrates often live in association this coral.

## BUSHY BLACK CORAL
*Antipathes n. sp.*
ORDER:
Antipatharia

**Bushy Colony**
[far left]
**Branch/Polyp Detail**
[near left]

SIZE: 2 - 12 ft.
DEPTH: 40 - 300 ft.

## FEATHER BLACK CORAL
*Antipathes pennacea*
ORDER:
Antipatharia

SIZE: 1 - 5 ft.
DEPTH: 15 - 1000 ft.

*continued next page*

**VISUAL ID:** Upright colonies of stiff, coarse, primary and secondary branches extend in nearly a single plane. Occasionally, somewhat bushy. Bright orangish brown to orange-red. (Similar Gray Sea Fan Black Coral [next] distinguished by gray to greenish color, with network of fine, delicate branches.)

**ABUNDANCE & DISTRIBUTION:** Occasional Bahamas, Caribbean; rare South Florida.

**HABITAT & BEHAVIOR:** Inhabit most deep environments, often at the base of walls or in the open on reef tops. Prefer areas with good water circulation. Generally inhabit more open areas than similar Gray Sea Fan Black Coral [next].

**Sparsely Branched Colony**

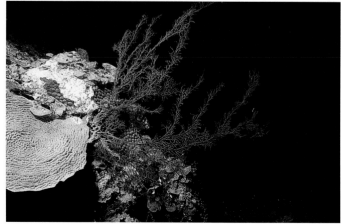

**Branchlet/Polyp Detail**

**Grayish Variety**
[far left]
**Golden Brown Variety**
[near left]

ORANGE SEA FAN
BLACK CORAL

ORANGE SEA FAN
BLACK CORAL
*Antipathes gracilis*
ORDER:
Antipatharia

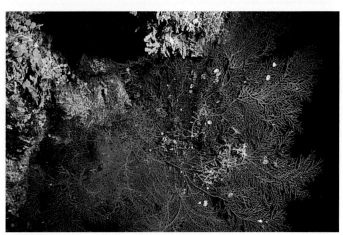

SIZE: 1$^{1}/_{2}$ - 4 ft.
DEPTH: 60 - 300 ft.

**Unusual
Thickly Branched
Colony**

**VISUAL ID:** Colonies shaped like large, classic sea fans with radiating primary branches and a network of numerous, fine, delicate, occasionally interconnecting secondary branches. Polyps shades of pale gray, sometimes tinged with pink, to greenish gray and dark gray; branches black. (Similar Orange Sea Fan Black Coral [previous] distinguished by bright orangish brown to red-brown color, and heavier, coarser, more bushy branches.)

**ABUNDANCE & DISTRIBUTION:** Occasional Bahamas, Caribbean; rare South Florida.

**HABITAT & BEHAVIOR:** Inhabit shaded deep reef environments, especially in canyons, crevices, under ledge overhangs and along walls where there is good water circulation. Generally more recluse than similar Orange Sea Fan Black Coral [previous].

**Unusually Bushy Colony**

**VISUAL ID:** Colonies form highly, subdivided tangled networks of fine branches that contour to the substrate. (Similar Scraggly Black Coral [next] distinguished by thicker, rigid, coarse branches.) Colonies do not protrude more than an inch or so above the substrate. Shades of brown to gray.

**ABUNDANCE & DISTRIBUTION:** Common Bahamas, Caribbean; occasional to uncommon South Florida.

**HABITAT & BEHAVIOR:** Inhabit shaded areas under ledge overhangs, cave ceilings and recessed wall faces.

**NOTE:** Pictured specimen collected (USNM 92277) at 90 feet, off Roatan, Honduras; visual identification confirmed by laboratory examination.

### GRAY SEA FAN
### BLACK CORAL
*Antipathes atlantica*
ORDER:
Antipatharia

SIZE: 1¹/₂ - 4 ft.
DEPTH: 60 - 300 ft.

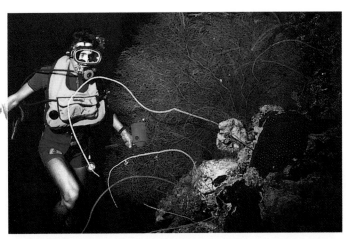

**Note Delicate**
**Net-like Structure**

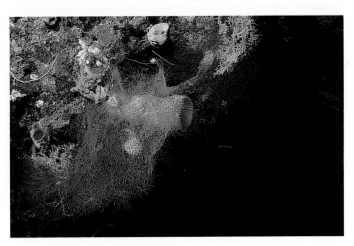

### HAIR NET
### BLACK CORAL
*Antipathes lenta*
ORDER:
Antipatharia

SIZE: 4 - 10 in.
DEPTH: 80 - 250 ft.

**VISUAL ID:** Colonies, with a single holdfast, form bramble bush-like tangles of rigid, coarse branches that contour to the substrate. (Similar Hair Net Black Coral [previous] distinguished by finer, more flexible branches.) Colonies do not protrude more than an inch or so above the substrate. Stalk structures gray to black; expanded polyp tentacles pale to translucent.

**ABUNDANCE & DISTRIBUTION:** Common Caribbean, Bahamas.

**HABITAT & BEHAVIOR:** Inhabit shaded areas under ledge overhangs, cave ceilings and undercut wall faces.

**NOTE:** Although these colonies are well known they have yet to be scientifically described. Pictured specimen collected (USNM 92274) at 90 feet, off Roatan, Honduras; visual identification confirmed by laboratory examination.

---

**VISUAL ID:** Bushy, upright colonies formed by openly branched primary and secondary stalks. (Similar Scraggly Bottle-brush [next] is more sparsely branched.) Numerous pinnules extend radially from stalks. Primary pinnules both long and short. There are occasional secondary pinnules, but tertiary pinnules are rare. Shades of gray to greenish gray and olive. Young colonies may have only a single, unbranched stalk and require microscopic examination for positive identification.

**ABUNDANCE & DISTRIBUTION:** Occasional to uncommon Florida, Bahamas, Caribbean.

**HABITAT & BEHAVIOR:** Deep reefs and gently sloping drop-offs.

---

**VISUAL ID:** Colonies formed by sparsely branched primary and secondary stalks. (Similar Bottle-brush Bush [previous] is more heavily branched.) Numerous pinnules extend radially from stalks. Primary pinnules long and generally of equal length. There are occasional secondary pinnules, but tertiary pinnules are rare. Shades of gray. Young colonies may have only single, unbranched stalks. (Note: colony pictured is young and just starting to branch near base.)

**ABUNDANCE & DISTRIBUTION:** Occasional to uncommon Florida, Bahamas, Caribbean.

**HABITAT & BEHAVIOR:** Inhabit deep reefs and gently sloping drop-offs; occasionally in old shipwrecks.

**NOTE:** Positive identification requires microscopic examination. Pictured specimen collected (USNM 92278) at 90 feet, off West Palm Beach, Florida and visual identification confirmed in laboratory.

### SCRAGGLY BLACK CORAL
*Antipathes n.* sp.
ORDER:
Antipatharia

SIZE: 6 - 12 in.
DEPTH: 60 - 250 ft.

### BOTTLE-BRUSH BUSH BLACK CORAL
*Antipathes hirta*
ORDER:
Antipatharia

SIZE: 1 - 2 ½ ft.
Pinnules 1 - 2 in.
DEPTH: 90 - 200 ft.

### SCRAGGLY BOTTLE-BRUSH BLACK CORAL
*Antipathes barbadensis*
ORDER:
Antipatharia

SIZE: 1 - 2 ft.
Pinnules 2 in.
DEPTH: 90 - 200 ft.

185

**VISUAL ID:** Colonies formed by long, unbranched primary stalks, from which numerous pinnules extend radially. Both secondary and tertiary pinnules common, giving the stalks a bushier appearance than Bottle-brush Bush [previous page middle] or Scraggly Bottle-brush [previous]. Colonies may be solitary, but often grow in clusters. Shades of gray.

**ABUNDANCE & DISTRIBUTION:** Occasional to uncommon Florida, Bahamas, Caribbean.

**HABITAT & BEHAVIOR:** Inhabit deep reefs and drop-offs; occasionally in old shipwrecks.

**NOTE:** Positive identification requires microscopic examination. Pictured specimen collected (USNM 92279) at 90 feet, off West Palm Beach, Florida; visual identification confirmed in laboratory.

---

**VISUAL ID:** Colonies form long, single, unbranched, wire-like stalks that often twist and coil. May appear fuzzy, the result of polyp tentacles extending from stalk surfaces. Shades of yellow, yellow-brown, red-brown, brown and green. Without artificial light, some colonies appear chartreuse.

**ABUNDANCE & DISTRIBUTION:** Common South Florida, Bahamas, Caribbean.

**HABITAT & BEHAVIOR:** Inhabit a wide range of deep water environments, but most common in narrow, deep-cut canyons and along vertical wall faces. May appear as the predominant life form on some deep walls. Most abundant at depths over 90 feet.

**NOTE:** Originally described in the genus *Stichopathes* which was subsequently recognized as a subgenus of *Cirrhipathes*.

**Branch/Polyp Detail of Red Variety**

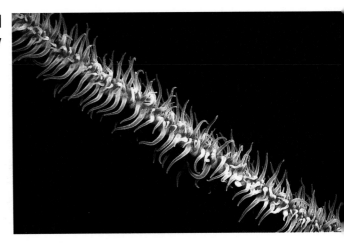

**BOTTLE-BRUSH
BLACK CORAL**
*Antipathes tanacetum*
ORDER:
Antipatharia

SIZE: 4 - 10 in.
Pinnules $^3/_4$ - $1^1/_2$ in.
DEPTH: 85 - 250 ft.

**WIRE CORAL**
*Cirrhipathes
(Stichopathes) leutkeni*
ORDER:
Antipatharia

SIZE: $1^1/_2$ - 14 ft.
DEPTH: 45 - 375 ft.

# Kingdom Plantae
# Kingdom Protista

## Marine Plants & Algae

Marine plants and algae (primarily phytoplankton) form the base of the oceanic food chain. All are photosynthetic, taking energy from sunlight and nutrients from the water or substrate, producing the food and oxygen used (either directly or indirectly) by other organisms to sustain life. Because they require sunlight for their vital processes, most grow intertidally to just over 100 feet. A few species grow deeper, and in the extremely clear water of the Caribbean some species may be found at surprising depths. There are over 600 species reported in the western tropical Atlantic. Those included in this text are the more common species growing on coral reefs and adjacent environments.

Marine plants, like their terrestrial counterparts, have true roots (containing conductive tissue), stems, leaves and flowers. Algae (singular alga) have no true roots, but attach to the substrate by holdfast structures called **rhizoids**, and runners connecting upright blades, called **rhizomes**. The upright parts of the plant are called **stalks** rather than stems, and **blades** instead of leaves. Several species of algae have bulb-like structures containing gas, called **bladders or floats**, that keep the structure upright. Most common marine algae can be visually identified by the shape of their blades and branching pattern. Algae are classified into Phyla on the basis of their predominate photosynthetic pigment. Although all contain some chlorophyll, only one group of algae is green.

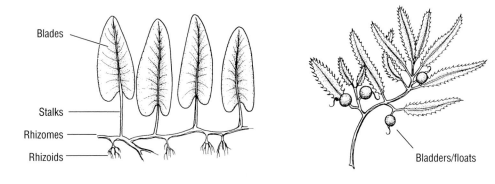

Blades

Stalks
Rhizomes
Rhizoids

Bladders/floats

## FLOWERING PLANTS

### Class Angiospermae (AN-gih-oo-sperm-uh/Gr. vessel and seed)

There are only a few species of marine flowering plants. Those most commonly observed by divers are the sea grasses (not related to terrestrial grasses) that often grow in great beds in areas of sand and sandy rubble adjacent to reefs. There are only three species, and each can be easily distinguished by the size and shape of its leaves.

# BROWN ALGAE

### Phylum Phaeophyta (Fay-OH-fita/Gr. dusky plant)

The two best known algae are both brown: Kelp, which grows primarily in the temperate latitudes of western North and South America; and Sargassum of the tropical and subtropical latitudes of the western Atlantic. Gas filled floats keep kelp upright and Sargassum floating on the surface. Brown algae ranges in color from shades of pale creamy brown to yellow-brown, green-brown and dark brown. Occasionally they are marked with shades of yellow, green and/or blue. Color is primarily the result of a brown pigment called fucoxanthin. Several species of brown algae are common inhabitants of the reef.

# GREEN ALGAE

### Phylum Chlorophyta (Klor-OH-fita/Gr. green plant)

Generally the most commonly observed algae on tropical reefs are green. They are both abundant and represented by a large number of species. Many are calcareous and along with coralline red algae add significant amounts of calcium carbonate to the reefs, as well as, much of the brilliant white sand found on and around reefs. Green algae grow in a wide range of patterns, including single-celled bubble-like plants to fan-like blades, bristly brushes, hanging vines and serrated edged, upright blades. Chlorophyll is the pigment primarily responsible for their color, which ranges from shades of pale mint green to bright Kelly green, yellowish-green, brownish-green and dark green.

# RED ALGAE

### Phylum Rhodophyta (Rode-OH-fita/Gr. rose-red plant)

Red algae, although abundant on tropical reefs, often goes unnoticed because of their generally dull coloration and nondescript growth forms. They are the most diversified of the algae, with over 4,000 tropical species. Calcareous species are important and integral elements in the reef building process. Many of those adding calcium carbonate to the reef are encrusting and appear as nothing more than a dull red to lavender to purple coloration of the rocky substrate. Reef crests exposed to vigorous wave activity are often thoroughly cemented by the activity of calcareous red algae, forming a reef zone called the algal ridge. Algal ridges can be found along the exposed reefs of the Windward Islands, Panama and St. Croix. Many noncoralline red algae are weed-like, growing in reddish translucent tangles, while others appear mossy or fuzzy. The primary red-pink pigment phycoerythrin, in combination with other pigments, is responsible for colors that range from pale pink to lavender, purple, brown-red and dark burgundy red.

# Sea Grasses

**VISUAL ID:** Generally erect, flat, ribbon-shaped, green leaves with rounded tips. Have extensive root system with well anchored runners. Produce pale pink to greenish white flowers. Leaves often covered with sediment and encrusting organisms.

**ABUNDANCE & DISTRIBUTION:** Abundant Florida, Bahamas, Caribbean.

**HABITAT & BEHAVIOR:** Grow on sandy bottoms and areas of mixed sand and coral rubble. Form beds, often covering extensive areas. Most common between 0-35 feet.

**Thickly Packed Beds Can Cover Large Areas**

**VISUAL ID:** Generally erect, thin, stem-like, cylindrical, green leaves. Have extensive network of runners. Leaves often covered with sediment and encrusting organisms

**ABUNDANCE & DISTRIBUTION:** Common Florida, Bahamas, Caribbean.

**HABITAT & BEHAVIOR:** Grow on sandy bottoms and areas of mixed sand and coral rubble. Form beds that commonly spread over extensive areas. Often mixed in with Turtle Grass.

### TURTLE GRASS
*Thalassia testudinum*
Class:
Angiospermae

SIZE: Length 4 - 24 in.
Width $1/8$ - $1/2$ in.
DEPTH: 3 - 65 ft.

**Widely Space Plants, Mixed with Manatee Grass** [next]

### MANATEE GRASS
*Syringodium filiforme*
CLASS:
Angiospermae

SIZE: Length $1^1/2$ - 18 in.
DEPTH: 3 - 40 ft.

**VISUAL ID:** Generally erect, flat, elongated-oval, green leaves with distinctive midribs. Leaves of older, taller specimens are often rippled. Have extensive root system with well anchored runners. Leaves often covered with sediment and encrusting organisms.

**ABUNDANCE & DISTRIBUTION:** Occasional Florida, Bahamas, Caribbean.

**HABITAT & BEHAVIOR:** Grow in a wide range of habitats from muddy bottoms to sandy areas adjacent to reefs. May occur in areas of high sedimentation. Grow deeper than other sea grasses.

---

**VISUAL ID:** Individual plants join to form dense, relatively thick, floating mats that can cover huge areas of the sea surface. Thin, smooth, branching stems bear long, serrated blades and spherical, gas-filled floats that keep the plants on the surface. (Similar Sargasso Weed [next] distinguished by small spine or hook-like projection on floats). Light yellow-brown to golden brown to brown. Blades have distinctive central veins of lighter color.

**ABUNDANCE & DISTRIBUTION:** Abundant to common South Florida, Bahamas, Caribbean.

**HABITAT & BEHAVIOR:** Free floating on open sea surface. May form small clumps or huge rafts covering enormous areas of the ocean. Usually mixed with Sargasso Weed [next].

**NOTE:** Also commonly known as "Gulf Weed."

**Surface View of Floating Sargassum Seaweed and Sargasso Weed**

## MIDRIB SEAGRASS
*Halophila baillonis*
CLASS:
Angiospermae

SIZE: Length 1 - 2 in.
DEPTH: 12 - 90 ft.

## SARGASSUM SEAWEED
*Sargassum fluitans*
PHYLUM:
Phaeophyta
**Brown Algae**

SIZE: ¹/₂ - 1¹/₂ ft.
DEPTH: 0 - 3 ft.

**Large Floating Mat
of Sargassum Seaweed
and Sargasso Weed**

**VISUAL ID:** Individual plants join to form dense, relatively thick, floating mats that can cover huge areas of the sea surface. Thin, branching stems with small spines bear long, thin, serrated blades without prominent central veins. Spherical, gas-filled floats, tipped with small spines or hook-like projections, keep the plants on the surface. (Similar Sargassum Seaweed [previous] distinguished by floats without prominent spines and blades with obvious central veins.) Antique white to pale brown.

**ABUNDANCE & DISTRIBUTION:** Abundant to common South Florida, Bahamas, Caribbean.

**HABITAT & BEHAVIOR:** Free floating on open sea surface. May form small clumps or huge rafts covering enormous areas of the ocean. Usually mixed with Sargassum Seaweed [previous].

---

**VISUAL ID:** Several species of *Sargassum* attach to the substrate and grow in a bushy, upright form. Long, oval-shaped blades may have smooth or striated edges. Blades along with clusters of spherical gas-filled floats are attached to smooth, cylindrical stems. Whitish brown to brown, brown-green and olive. The similarity between species requires collection and laboratory examination for positive identification.

**ABUNDANCE & DISTRIBUTION:** Common to occasional South Florida, Bahamas, Caribbean.

**HABITAT & BEHAVIOR:** Grow in most environments, including reefs.

### SARGASSO WEED
*Sargassum natans*
PHYLUM:
Phaeophyta
**Brown Algae**

SIZE: ¹/₂ - 1¹/₂ ft.
DEPTH: 0 - 3 ft.

### SARGASSUM ALGAE
*Sargassum* sp.
PHYLUM:
Phaeophyta
**Brown Algae**

SIZE: 4 in. - 5 ft.
DEPTH: 1 - 100 ft.

# Brown Algae

**VISUAL ID:** Long, oval-shaped leaves are shades of brown to dark olive and distinctively marked with white central veins. Leaves attached to smooth, cylindrical stems. Can be somewhat bushy.

**ABUNDANCE & DISTRIBUTION:** Common to occasional South Florida, Bahamas, Caribbean.

**HABITAT & BEHAVIOR:** Grow in most environments, including reefs. Most common on deep patch reefs and surrounding areas of sand and rocky substrate.

---

**VISUAL ID:** There are several species in this genus difficult to distinguish visually, some described, others undescribed. All have branches that fork near their ends. Tips may be rounded or pointed. Generally they form mats of dense to loose packed flat leaves that overgrow the substrate. Light to medium brown and/or green to blue-green, occasionally with bright blue tints. Can spread to cover large areas.

**ABUNDANCE & DISTRIBUTION:** Abundant South Florida, Bahamas, Caribbean.

**HABITAT & BEHAVIOR:** Grow in most reef environments. Grow on rocky substrates, often covering boulders, around the base of coral heads, and on vertical wall faces. Most common in protected areas.

**NOTE:** Described species include *D. cervicornis, bartayresii, linearis* and *divaricata*.

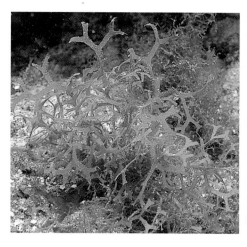

### WHITE-VEIN SARGASSUM
*Sargassum hystrix*
PHYLUM:
Phaeophyta
**Brown Algae**

SIZE: 4 - 16 in.
DEPTH: 30 - 330 ft.

### Y BRANCHED ALGAE
*Dictyota* sp.
PHYLUM:
Phaeophyta
**Brown Algae**

SIZE: 4 - 18 in.
DEPTH: 0 - 200 ft.

**VISUAL ID:** Bushy clumps of strap-like blades that have distinctive points along their edges. Irregularly branched dichotomously. Light yellow-brown to brown, with light, wavy pattern; may have greenish tints.

**ABUNDANCE & DISTRIBUTION:** Abundant South Florida, Bahamas, Caribbean.

**HABITAT & BEHAVIOR:** Grow in most reef environments. Attach to rocky substrates, often in exposed areas with surge.

**SIMILAR SPECIES:** Smooth Strap Algae, *D. dichotoma*, distinguished by thin, dichotomously branched blades with smooth edges.

---

**VISUAL ID:** Bushy plant formed by flat, squared-off blades that are irregularly branched and split. Concentrically banded in a wide range of colors, including shades of yellow, yellow-green, green, brown-green, brown, and often with tints of iridescent green and/or blue.

**ABUNDANCE & DISTRIBUTION:** Abundant to occasional South Florida, Bahamas, Caribbean.

**HABITAT & BEHAVIOR:** Attach to rocky substrate in most reef environments. Often abundant in shallow water less than five feet, only occasional to rare on deeper reefs.

## SERRATED STRAP ALGA
*Dictyota ciliolata*
PHYLUM:
Phaeophyta
**Brown Algae**

SIZE: 4 - 6 in.
DEPTH: 0 - 35 ft.

## LEAFY FLAT-BLADE ALGA
*Stypopodium zonale*
PHYLUM:
Phaeophyta
**Brown Algae**

SIZE: Blade length
3$^1/_2$ - 16 in.
DEPTH: 0 - 260 ft.

### Color Varieties

# Brown Algae

**VISUAL ID:** Form large, dense clumps of leafy blades with rounded, often semicircular outer margins. Blades are irregularly split and branched. Concentrically banded in a wide range of colors, including shades of yellow, yellow-green, green, brown-green, brown, and often with tints of iridescent green and/or blue. Outer margins are often of lighter color.

**ABUNDANCE & DISTRIBUTION:** Abundant to occasional South Florida, Bahamas, Caribbean.

**HABITAT & BEHAVIOR:** Attach to rocky substrate in most reef environments. Often abundant in shallow water less than five feet, while only occasional to rare on deeper reefs.

**NOTE:** Identification tentative; members of this genus require sectioning near the base and microscopic examination for positive identification. Formerly classified as *P. gymnospora.*

---

**VISUAL ID:** Form large, dense clumps of leafy blades with rounded, often semicircular, outer margins. Blades are irregularly split and branched. Concentrically banded in shades of white to grayish white, tan and light yellowish brown.

**ABUNDANCE & DISTRIBUTION:** Abundant to occasional South Florida, Bahamas, Caribbean.

**HABITAT & BEHAVIOR:** Attach to rocky substrates in most marine environments, especially shallow reef flats.

**NOTE:** Identification tentative; members of this genus require sectioning near the base and microscopic examination for positive identification. Formerly classified as *P. sanctae-crucis.*

---

**VISUAL ID:** Thin, fan-shaped blades encrust substrate, often overlapping in a shingle-like pattern. Shades of green-brown to tan to brown.

**ABUNDANCE & DISTRIBUTION:** Abundant to common South Florida, Bahamas, Caribbean.

**HABITAT & BEHAVIOR:** Grow in most reef environments, encrusting great areas of shaded, rocky substrate. Especially abundant on undercut wall faces along deep drop-offs. Blade surfaces often covered with sediment and encrusted with other growths (epiphytes).

**NOTE:** This species has two additional growth forms; both grow in shallow to intertidal water and rarely on reefs. The blades of both forms are less flattened and more ruffled and range in color from light green to orange-brown.

### LEAFY ROLLED-BLADE ALGA
*Padina boergesenii*
PHYLUM:
Phaeophyta
**Brown Algae**

SIZE: Blade length
4 - 6 in.
DEPTH: 0 - 50 ft.

### WHITE SCROLL ALGA
*Padina jamaicensis*
PHYLUM:
Phaeophyta
**Brown Algae**

SIZE: Blade height
2¹/₂ - 6 in.
DEPTH: 0 - 50 ft.

### ENCRUSTING FAN-LEAF ALGA
*Lobophora variegata*
PHYLUM:
Phaeophyta
**Brown Algae**

SIZE: Blade diameter
1 - 6 in.
DEPTH: 12 - 350 ft.

# Brown Algae

**VISUAL ID:** A spongy-looking mass of tangled, interconnected branches with numerous irregularly sized holes. Has no permanent holdfasts and can form large masses. Very pale brown to light yellow-brown. May fluoresce dayglow orange which disappears when illuminated by a hand light or strobe.

**ABUNDANCE & DISTRIBUTION:** Abundant to common Florida; occasional to rare Bahamas, Caribbean.

**HABITAT & BEHAVIOR:** Grow in most reef environments. May move about in current, coming to rest in shallow depressions or where the mass hooks on or around various bottom growths or outcroppings.

---

**VISUAL ID:** Erect central column with branches bearing clumps of triangular, cone-shaped blades with saucer-like tips. (Similar Blistered Saucer Leaf Alga [next] leaf tips have swollen centers.) Short, sharp spines extend from blade stalk. Brownish cream to tan to brown, often with dark brown speckles.

**ABUNDANCE & DISTRIBUTION:** Occasional Florida, Bahamas, Caribbean.

**HABITAT & BEHAVIOR:** Grow in shallow intertidal zones to shallow lagoons and back reef areas with moderate to strong water movement.

**NOTE:** This species and Blistered Saucer Leaf Alga [next] are so similar in appearance that positive identification requires collection and laboratory examination.

---

**VISUAL ID:** Erect central column with branches bearing clumps of triangular, cone-shaped blades with saucer-like tips. A blister-like swelling at center of leaf tips is the result of an embedded air bladder that holds the leaves and plant erect (compare similar Saucer Leaf Alga [previous]). Brownish cream to tan to brown, often with dark brown speckles.

**ABUNDANCE & DISTRIBUTION:** Occasional Florida, Bahamas, Caribbean.

**HABITAT & BEHAVIOR:** Grow in shallow intertidal zones to shallow lagoons and back reef areas with moderate to strong water movement.

**NOTE:** This species and Saucer Leaf Alga [previous] are so similar in appearance that positive identification requires collection and laboratory examination.

### SWISS CHEESE ALGA
*Hydroclathrus clathratus*
PHYLUM:
Phaeophyta
**Brown Algae**

SIZE: 3 in. - 3 ft.
DEPTH: 10 - 60 ft.

### SAUCER LEAF ALGA
*Turbinaria tricostata*
PHYLUM:
Phaeophyta
**Brown Algae**

SIZE: 4 - 16 in.
DEPTH: 0 - 20 ft.

### BLISTERED SAUCER LEAF ALGA
*Turbinaria turbinata*
PHYLUM:
Phaeophyta
**Brown Algae**

SIZE: 4 - 16 in.
DEPTH: 0 - 20 ft.

# Green Algae

**VISUAL ID:** Thick, profusely branched clumps of rounded, three-lobed or ribbed, leaf-like segments. Spread laterally to cover large areas of reef or sand. Dark to bright green and yellowish green.

**ABUNDANCE & DISTRIBUTION:** Abundant South Florida, Bahamas, Caribbean.

**HABITAT & BEHAVIOR:** Grow in shallow depressions, cracks and crevices, between hard corals and other somewhat protected areas of the reef. Also grow on sand, especially around and on reefs.

**NOTE:** The calcified leaves of this and other species of *Halimeda* are considered major contributors of calcium carbonate to the reefs and sand.

**Can Cover
Large Areas
of Reef**

**VISUAL ID:** Branched clumps of rounded, smooth, fan- or disk-shaped, leaf-like segments. Attached by single, short holdfast with flexible joints between segments. Tend to grow in single plane (less obvious in larger plants). Bright green to yellowish green, occasionally white; segment edges often yellow. Leaf-like segments are the largest found in this genus.

**ABUNDANCE & DISTRIBUTION:** Abundant to common South Florida, Bahamas, Caribbean.

**HABITAT & BEHAVIOR:** Grow in most marine environments from reefs to flat bottom plains of sand, rubble and hard substrates.

**NOTE:** The calcified leaves of this and other species of *Halimeda* are considered major contributors of calcium carbonate to the reefs and sand.

## WATERCRESS ALGA
*Halimeda opuntia*
PHYLUM:
Chlorophyta
**Green Algae**

SIZE: 4 - 8 in.
Segment width
¹/₈ - ³/₈ in.
DEPTH: 3 - 150 ft.

**Note White Calcareous Structure of Dead Segments**

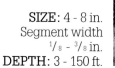

## LARGE LEAF WATERCRESS ALGA
*Halimeda discoidea*
PHYLUM:
Chlorophyta
**Green Algae**

SIZE: 4 - 8 in.
Segment width
³/₈ - 1¹/₂ in.
DEPTH: 3 - 220 ft.

# Green Algae

**VISUAL ID:** Branched clumps of thin, rounded, fan- or disk-shaped, leaf-like segments. Attached by stalk formed of basal segments, especially noticeable in older plants. Young tend to grow in single plane, becoming somewhat bushy with age. Bright green to yellowish green, and green.

**ABUNDANCE & DISTRIBUTION:** Abundant to common South Florida, Bahamas, Caribbean.

**HABITAT & BEHAVIOR:** Grow in most marine environments from reefs to flat bottom plains of sand, rubble and hard substrates.

**NOTE:** The calcified leaves of this and other species of *Halimeda* are considered major contributors of calcium carbonate to the reefs and sand.

---

**VISUAL ID:** Chains of spherical or bulbous segments, resembling strings of beads, without distinct stalk. Pale green to whitish.

**ABUNDANCE & DISTRIBUTION:** Common to occasional South Florida, Bahamas, Cuba. Not reported Caribbean.

**HABITAT & BEHAVIOR:** Grow on reefs and rocky substrates.

**NOTE:** The calcified leaves of this and other species of *Halimeda* are considered major contributors of calcium carbonate to the reefs and sand.

---

**VISUAL ID:** Long chain of rounded, three-lobed, relatively small, leaf-like segments held together by a thin strand running through their centers. Rare to occasional branching of strands. Bright green to yellowish green.

**ABUNDANCE & DISTRIBUTION:** Abundant to common South Florida, Bahamas, Caribbean.

**HABITAT & BEHAVIOR:** Tend to grow in shaded areas of reef, often hanging from ledge undercuts and along walls.

**NOTE:** The calcified leaves of this and other species of *Halimeda* are considered major contributors of calcium carbonate to the reefs and sand.

## STALKED LETTUCE LEAF ALGA
*Halimeda tuna*
PHYLUM:
Chlorophyta
**Green Algae**

SIZE: 4 - 10 in.
Segment width
$^{1}/_{2}$ - $^{3}/_{4}$ in.
DEPTH: 30 - 220 ft.

## BULBOUS LETTUCE LEAF ALGA
*Halimeda lacrimosa*
PHYLUM:
Chlorophyta
**Green Algae**

SIZE: Height 1 - 2 in.
Chain length to 10 in.
Segment diameter $^{1}/_{4}$ in.
DEPTH: 3 - 280 ft.

## SMALL-LEAF HANGING VINE
*Halimeda goreaui*
PHYLUM:
Chlorophyta
**Green Algae**

SIZE: Strand length
6 - 12 in.
Segment width
$^{1}/_{8}$ - $^{1}/_{4}$ in.
DEPTH: 30 - 250 ft.

# Green Algae

**VISUAL ID:** Long chain of rectangular-shaped, relatively large, leaf-like segments held together by a thin strand running through their centers. Strands may branch frequently. Bright green to yellowish green on top, underside often lighter.

**ABUNDANCE & DISTRIBUTION:** Abundant to common South Florida, Bahamas, Caribbean.

**HABITAT & BEHAVIOR:** Tend to grow in shaded areas of reef, often hanging from ledge undercuts and along walls.

**NOTE:** The calcified leaves of this and other species of *Halimeda* are considered major contributors of calcium carbonate to the reefs and sand.

---

**VISUAL ID:** Upright, occasionally branched, chains of distinctly three-lobed or ribbed, leaf-like segments. Stiff, primary stalk composed of united segments. Dark to bright green to yellowish green.

**ABUNDANCE & DISTRIBUTION:** Abundant to common South Florida, Bahamas, Caribbean.

**HABITAT & BEHAVIOR:** Most commonly inhabit shallow sandy areas, including sea grass beds. Occasionally in sandy, rocky areas on and between reefs.

**NOTE:** The calcified leaves of this and other species of *Halimeda* are considered major contributors of calcium carbonate to the reefs and sand.

## LARGE-LEAF HANGING VINE
*Halimeda copiosa*
PHYLUM:
Chlorophyta
**Green Algae**

SIZE: Strand length
4 - 24 in.
Segment width $^1/_2$ - $^3/_4$ in.
DEPTH: 50 - 200 ft.

**Detail of Leaf-like Segments**

## THREE FINGER LEAF ALGA
*Halimeda incrassata*
PHYLUM:
Chlorophyta
**Green Algae**

SIZE: Height 4 - 10 in.
DEPTH: 3 - 40 ft.

**VISUAL ID:** Upright, occasionally branched, chains of cylindrical to somewhat flattened segments. Branching occurs from three-lobed segments. Relatively stiff structure. Dark to bright green to yellowish green.

**ABUNDANCE & DISTRIBUTION:** Occasional South Florida, Bahamas, Caribbean.

**HABITAT & BEHAVIOR:** Most commonly inhabit shallow sandy areas, including sea grass beds. Occasionally in sandy, rocky areas on and between reefs.

**NOTE:** The calcified leaves of this and other species of *Halimeda* are considered major contributors of calcium carbonate to the reefs and sand.

---

**VISUAL ID:** Cone-shaped with flattish top. Tip of cone merges into a heavy, short stalk anchored in sand. Composed of tightly packed, bristle-like filaments. Dark green to gray-green.

**ABUNDANCE & DISTRIBUTION:** Occasional South Florida, Bahamas, Caribbean.

**HABITAT & BEHAVIOR:** Grow in sandy, protected areas, often on and between reefs.

**NOTE:** Identification probable, positive identification requires collection and laboratory examination.

---

**VISUAL ID:** Spherical ball of tightly packed bristle-like filaments that merge into a heavy, short stalk anchored in sand. Composed of tightly packed, bristle-like filaments. Dark green to gray-green.

**ABUNDANCE & DISTRIBUTION:** Occasional South Florida, Bahamas, Caribbean.

**HABITAT & BEHAVIOR:** Grow in sandy, protected areas, often on and between reefs.

### GREEN JOINTED-STALK ALGA
*Halimeda monile*
PHYLUM:
Chlorophyta
**Green Algae**

SIZE: Height 3 - 8 in.
DEPTH: 3 - 40 ft.

### FLAT-TOP BRISTLE BRUSH
*Penicillus pyriformis*
PHYLUM:
Chlorophyta
**Green Algae**

SIZE: 2 - 4 ½ in.
DEPTH: 3 - 100 ft.

### BRISTLE BALL BRUSH
*Penicillus dumetosus*
PHYLUM:
Chlorophyta
**Green Algae**

SIZE: 2 - 6 in.
DEPTH: 6 - 50 ft.

# Green Algae

**VISUAL ID:** Tall, stiff, feather-like structures grow upward from long, cylindrical, attached runners. Pinnate branchlets are cylindrical with sharp points. Light green.

**ABUNDANCE & DISTRIBUTION:** Occasional South Florida, Bahamas, Caribbean.

**HABITAT & BEHAVIOR:** Grow in shallow sandy areas, often between protected shallow reefs. Also grow in areas of mangroves and occasionally attach to their roots.

---

**VISUAL ID:** Flat feather-like structures grow upward from long, cylindrical, attached runners. Pinnate branchlets have sharp points and taper into the midrib. Yellow-green to green.

**ABUNDANCE & DISTRIBUTION:** Occasional South Florida, Bahamas, Caribbean.

**HABITAT & BEHAVIOR:** Grow in shallow to moderate depths in sandy areas and on rocky reefs. Also grow in areas of mangroves and occasionally attach to their roots. In shallow areas with surge, tend to be short (about 1-3 inches); reach maximum height in deeper protected areas.

---

**VISUAL ID:** Small serrated blades with edges grow upward from long, cylindrical, attached runners. Blades often fork and are occasionally twisted. Shades of light to medium mint green, often with bluish tints.

**ABUNDANCE & DISTRIBUTION:** Occasional South Florida, Bahamas, Caribbean.

**HABITAT & BEHAVIOR:** Grow in shallow rocky substrates, usually with some sand covering. Often adjacent to protected back patch and fringing reefs.

### GREEN FEATHER ALGA
*Caulerpa sertularioides*
PHYLUM:
Chlorophyta
**Green Algae**

SIZE: 4 - 8 in.
DEPTH: 3 - 35 ft.

### FLAT GREEN FEATHER ALGA
*Caulerpa mexicana*
PHYLUM:
Chlorophyta
**Green Algae**

SIZE: 1 - 8 in.
DEPTH: 3 - 50 ft.

### SAW-BLADE ALGA
*Caulerpa serrulata*
PHYLUM:
Chlorophyta
**Green Algae**

SIZE: Blades
³/₄ - 1¹/₂ in.
DEPTH: 3 - 18 ft.

**VISUAL ID:** Small, flat, elongated, oval blades with short, cylindrical stalks. Additional blades may branch off from stalk. Grow upward from long, cylindrical, attached runners. Yellow-green to green and dark green.

**ABUNDANCE & DISTRIBUTION:** Occasional South Florida, Bahamas, Caribbean.

**HABITAT & BEHAVIOR:** Grow in sandy areas, often adjacent to shallow patch reefs. May mix with Turtle Grass.

---

**VISUAL ID:** Numerous, long, branching, cylindrical runners bear clusters of grape-like spheres attached by tiny stem-like branchlets. Shades of light to medium green, often with bluish tints. Somewhat different growth patterns of this species, var. *peltata*, have disk-like appendages attached to the branchlets; var. *macrophyso*, form upright columns bearing grape-like spheres.

**ABUNDANCE & DISTRIBUTION:** Common South Florida, Bahamas, Caribbean.

**HABITAT & BEHAVIOR:** Most commonly grow in intertidal to shallow rocky areas, usually with at least some surge and water movement. Also inhabit rocky areas of shallow to moderately deep reefs. Several species of nudibranchs feed exclusively on this alga.

**Upright Column Growth Pattern, Var. *macrophyso***

**OVAL-BLADE ALGA**
*Caulerpa prolifera*
PHYLUM:
Chlorophyta
**Green Algae**

SIZE: Blades
2 - 4 in.
DEPTH: 3 - 50 ft.

**GREEN GRAPE ALGA**
*Caulerpa racemosa*
PHYLUM:
Chlorophyta
**Green Algae**

SIZE: $^1/_2$ - 6 in.
DEPTH: 0 - 65 ft.

**Disk-shaped Tip
Growth Pattern,
Var. *peltata***

**VISUAL ID:** Trunk-like stalks that divide into thick, heavy, upright branches extend from sand covered runners. Branches lined with long rows of short, thick, variously shaped branchlets. May be tall and slender with only a few branches, or short and bushy with numerous branches.

**ABUNDANCE & DISTRIBUTION:** Occasional South Florida, Bahamas, Caribbean. Can be abundant in localized areas.

**HABITAT & BEHAVIOR:** Grow in shallow, protected sandy areas, often adjacent to back patch and fringing reefs.

**SIMILAR SPECIES:** Tall Cactus Alga, *C. lanuginosa*, single, unbranched columns (3-5 in.) grow upward from sand-covered runners.

---

**VISUAL ID:** Small, cylindrical, ringed stalks with fuzzy tips. May grow singly or in compact clumps. Tips green; stalks white with greenish tints.

**ABUNDANCE & DISTRIBUTION:** Occasional South Florida, Bahamas, Caribbean. Can be abundant in localized areas.

**HABITAT & BEHAVIOR:** Grow on sandy, rocky substrates and areas of coral rubble. Occasionally on reefs. Often in shaded areas.

---

**VISUAL ID:** Clusters of cylindrical branches composed of fine, tightly compacted branchlets. Olive to dark green.

**ABUNDANCE & DISTRIBUTION:** Occasional South Florida, Bahamas, Caribbean.

**HABITAT & BEHAVIOR:** Grow in a variety of shallow water habitats, from mangrove areas to tidal pools to shallow reefs. Attach to hard substrates.

**NOTE:** Identification probable, positive identification requires collection and magnified examination of branchlet filaments.

### CACTUS TREE ALGA
*Caulerpa cupressoides*
PHYLUM:
Chlorophyta
**Green Algae**

SIZE: Height 1 - 10 in.
DEPTH: 3 - 18 ft.

### FUZZY TIP ALGA
*Neomeris annulata*
PHYLUM:
Chlorophyta
**Green Algae**

SIZE: Height $^3/_4$ - $1^1/_4$ in.
DEPTH: 0 - 100 ft.

### FUZZY FINGER ALGA
*Dasycladus vermicularis*
PHYLUM:
Chlorophyta
**Green Algae**

SIZE: Height 1 - $2^1/_2$ in.
DEPTH: 0 - 25 ft.

# Green Algae

**VISUAL ID:** Bushy, hemispherical growths of cylindrical branches with fine, hair-like covering. Branch tips often dichotomously branched. Pale to medium green.

**ABUNDANCE & DISTRIBUTION:** Occasional South Florida, Bahamas, Caribbean.

**HABITAT & BEHAVIOR:** Grow on rocky substrates, occasionally on reefs. Most common in shallow areas between 5-25 feet.

---

**VISUAL ID:** Dark green spheres with bright reflective sheen. Often covered with thin, silvery to light lavender alga. Attached to substrate by fine, hair-like runners. One of the largest single cells found in either the Plant or Animal Kingdoms.

**ABUNDANCE & DISTRIBUTION:** Common to occasional South Florida, Bahamas, Caribbean.

**HABITAT & BEHAVIOR:** Grow in most reef environments, often in small cracks and crevices mixed with other algae. Tend to be solitary, but occasionally in small groups. May be encrusted with tunicates and other organisms.

---

**VISUAL ID:** Dark green bubble-like cells with bright, reflective, silvery sheen. Range from spheres to elongated ovals. Grow in tightly compacted, mat-like clusters.

**ABUNDANCE & DISTRIBUTION:** Common South Florida, Bahamas, Caribbean.

**HABITAT & BEHAVIOR:** Inhabit most reef environments, especially in protected, shaded areas, such as under ledge overhangs and in cracks. Often overgrown by other organisms. More common on shallow reefs, but also occurs much deeper.

**NOTE:** There are several similar appearing species of *Valonia* and identification is tentative. Positive identification requires laboratory examination of collected specimen.

## DEAD MAN'S FINGERS
*Codium isthmocladum*
PHYLUM:
Chlorophyta
**Green Algae**

SIZE: Height 4 - 8 in.
DEPTH: 3 - 80 ft.

## SEA PEARL
*Ventricaria ventricosa*
PHYLUM:
Chlorophyta
**Green Algae**

SIZE: Diameter
$^3/_4$ - 2 in.
DEPTH: 3 - 250 ft.

## ELONGATED SEA PEARLS
*Valonia macrophysa*
PHYLUM:
Chlorophyta
**Green Algae**

SIZE: Diameter
$^1/_4$ - $^3/_4$ in.
DEPTH: 3 - 140 ft.

**VISUAL ID:** Clusters of dark green, bubble-like cells grow in spreading runners. Do not form dense mats as Elongated Sea Pearls [previous]. Shapes range from spheres to elongated ovals. Outgrowths are occasionally erect.

**ABUNDANCE & DISTRIBUTION:** Occasional South Florida, Bahamas, Caribbean.

**HABITAT & BEHAVIOR:** Inhabit most reef environments, especially in protected, shaded areas, such as under ledge overhangs and in cracks. Most common on shallow reefs, but also occur much deeper.

**NOTE:** There are several similar appearing species of *Valonia* and identification is tentative. Positive identification requires laboratory examination of collected specimen.

---

**VISUAL ID:** Spherical to irregularly lobed clumps. Walls composed of small bubble-like cells giving the surface a cobblestone-like texture. Shades of light green.

**ABUNDANCE & DISTRIBUTION:** Common to occasional South Florida, Bahamas, Caribbean.

**HABITAT & BEHAVIOR:** Grow in most reef environments, attaching to rocky substrates and areas of dead coral. On occasion cover extensive areas. Can be abundant in localized areas, especially with high nutrient levels.

---

**VISUAL ID:** Thin, rounded, upright blades composed of long vertical veins that divide at their tips into sprays of smaller veins, reminiscent of papyrus grass. Large, elongated cells lay parallel to one another between, and at 90-degree angles to, the veins. Shades of bright green to yellowish green.

**ABUNDANCE & DISTRIBUTION:** Occasional South Florida, Bahamas, Caribbean.

**HABITAT & BEHAVIOR:** Grow in shaded, protected, rocky areas such as under ledge overhangs and in cracks and crevices.

## CREEPING BUBBLE ALGA
*Valonia utricularis*
**PHYLUM:**
Chlorophyta
**Green Algae**

SIZE: Diameter ¹/₄ in.
Length to 1 in.
DEPTH: 3 - 100 ft.

## GREEN BUBBLE WEED
*Dictyosphaeria*
*cavernosa*
**PHYLUM:**
Chlorophyta
**Green Algae**

SIZE: 1¹/₄ - 8 in.
DEPTH: 3 - 100 ft.

## PAPYRUS PRINT ALGA
*Anadyomene stellata*
**PHYLUM:**
Chlorophyta
**Green Algae**

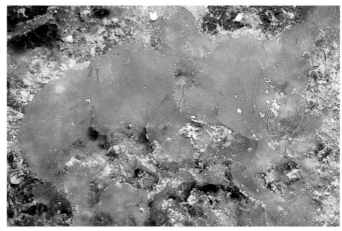

SIZE: 1¹/₄ - 4 in.
DEPTH: 0 - 100 ft.

# Green Algae

**VISUAL ID:** Clumps of thin, stiff, crumpled blades composed of a tight, rough network of long, large filaments. Pale to dark green.

**ABUNDANCE & DISTRIBUTION:** Occasional South Florida, Bahamas, Caribbean.

**HABITAT & BEHAVIOR:** Grow in open areas of reef attached to hard substrate. Often in environments with some light sedimentation.

**Close-up: Note Network Structure**

**VISUAL ID:** Tangled masses formed by a somewhat stiff network of long, fine filaments. Pale to dark green.

**ABUNDANCE & DISTRIBUTION:** Occasional Caribbean.

**HABITAT & BEHAVIOR:** Grow in most marine environments, more common in areas with little water movement. May attach in small clumps or grow in masses of considerable size, covering large areas of substrate.

**NOTE:** Visual identification probable, positive identification requires microscopic examination of collected specimen.

### NETWORK ALGA
*Microdictyon marinum*
PHYLUM:
Chlorophyta
**Green Algae**

SIZE: 1¹/₄ - 4 in.
DEPTH: 3 - 50 ft.

**Detail of
Filament Structure**

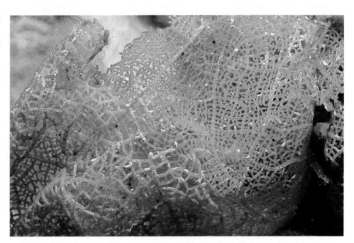

### GREEN NET ALGA
*Microdictyon
boergesenii*
PHYLUM:
Chlorophyta
**Green Algae**

SIZE: 1¹/₄ in. to
several ft.
DEPTH: 3 - 100 ft.

*continued next page*

# Green Algae

**Close-up of Network**

**VISUAL ID:** Fan-shaped blades with smooth edges and surface texture. Rounded bottom of blades turn in and upward to stem. Stems attached to long slender runners. Dark green to grayish green.

**ABUNDANCE & DISTRIBUTION:** Common to occasional South Florida, Bahamas, Caribbean.

**HABITAT & BEHAVIOR:** Grow in sandy areas, on and between reefs. In shallow areas with water movement, often in rows on short stalks. In deeper, calm water, often grow tall and singly or in small clusters.

**NOTE:** Identification probable, positive identification requires laboratory examination of collected specimen.

---

**VISUAL ID:** Paddle-shaped blades with relatively smooth edges and surface texture. Stems attached to large bulbous holdfast. Dark green to grayish green.

**ABUNDANCE & DISTRIBUTION:** Common to occasional South Florida, Bahamas, Caribbean.

**HABITAT & BEHAVIOR:** Grow in sandy areas, on and between reefs. In shallow areas with water movement, often in rows on short stalks. In deeper, calm water, often grow tall and singly or in small clusters.

**NOTE:** Identification probable, positive identification requires laboratory examination of collected specimen.

### GREEN NET ALGA
*continued from previous page*
**Detail of Structure**

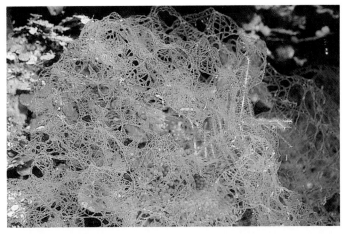

### SAUCER BLADE ALGA
*Avrainvillea asarifolia*
PHYLUM:
Chlorophyta
**Green Algae**

SIZE: Blade height
1¹/₂ - 6 in.
Stalk 1 - 12 in.
DEPTH: 3 - 120 ft.

### PADDLE BLADE ALGA
*Avrainvillea longicaulis*
PHYLUM:
Chlorophyta
**Green Algae**

SIZE: Blade height
1¹/₂ - 4 in.
Stalk 1 - 8 in.
DEPTH: 3 - 100 ft.

**VISUAL ID:** Several species in this genus have broad, fan-shaped blades attached to single stalks. They are heavily calcified, stiff and erect. Lines (thin filament ridges) extend radially from point of stem attachments to edge. Many have one or more concentric lines or zones on blades' surfaces. Whitish green to yellow-green, medium green and dark green. Because of their similarity in appearance, positive identification to species requires magnified examination of blade filaments.

**ABUNDANCE & DISTRIBUTION:** Common South Florida, Bahamas, Caribbean.

**HABITAT & BEHAVIOR:** Grow in sandy, protected areas, on and between reefs and areas of coral rubble. Usually grow in groups.

**NOTE:** Based on visual appearance of overall structure, opposite is possibly *U. flabellum*, middle right may be *U. spinulosa*, and bottom right may be *U. wilsonii*

## MERMAID'S FANS
*Udotea* sp.
PHYLUM:
Chlorophyta
**Green Algae**

SIZE: Height 1 - 8 in.
DEPTH: 0 - 120 ft.

**VISUAL ID:** Paper-thin cup attached to a small, single stalk anchored in sand. Quite delicate, structure often torn. Medium green to whitish green.

**ABUNDANCE & DISTRIBUTION:** Occasional South Florida, Bahamas, Caribbean.

**HABITAT & BEHAVIOR:** Grow in sandy, protected areas, on and between reefs and in areas of coral rubble. Usually grow in groups.

---

**VISUAL ID:** Pinecone-shaped, composed of tightly packed flattened blades growing upward and concentrically from a single stalk. Green to mint green and whitish green. There are two additional distinctive growth patterns of this species. Forma *brevifolius* has a thin, elongated pinecone shape. Forma *longifolius* has ragged, more loosely arranged blades and a somewhat flattened top.

**ABUNDANCE & DISTRIBUTION:** Occasional South Florida, Bahamas, Caribbean

**HABITAT & BEHAVIOR:** Most commonly inhabit shallow sandy areas, including sea grass beds. Occasionally in sandy, rocky areas on and between reefs.

**Elongate Pinecone Alga**
**forma *brevifolius***

## MERMAID'S TEA CUP
*Udotea cyathiformis*
PHYLUM:
Chlorophyta
**Green Algae**

SIZE: Cup height
2 - 6 in.
DEPTH: 3 - 100 ft.

## PINECONE ALGA
*Rhipocephalus phoenix*
PHYLUM:
Chlorophyta
**Green Algae**

SIZE: Height 2 - 5 in.
DEPTH: 3 - 150 ft.

**Ragged Pinecone Alga
forma *longifolius***

**VISUAL ID:** Round, saucer-shaped caps on long, thin stalks. Ruffled rays radiate from centers, with a small spine at the tip of each ray. White with slight greenish tint.

**ABUNDANCE & DISTRIBUTION:** Occasional South Florida, Bahamas, Caribbean.

**HABITAT & BEHAVIOR:** Grow in shallow protected areas of reef, areas of coral rubble, adjacent sea grass beds and mangrove areas. May grow solitary or in groups.

**NOTE:** Identification probable, positive identification requires microscopic examination of collected specimen.

---

**VISUAL ID:** Clumps of round, saucer-shaped caps on long thin stalks. Ruffled rays radiate from centers to edges. Pale green to yellowish green.

**ABUNDANCE & DISTRIBUTION:** Occasional South Florida, Bahamas, Caribbean.

**HABITAT & BEHAVIOR:** Grow in shallow protected areas of reef, areas of coral rubble, adjacent sea grass beds, sand flats and mangrove areas. Usually in clumps, rarely solitary.

**NOTE:** Identification probable, positive identification requires collection and microscopic examination.

---

**VISUAL ID:** Light pink color is distinctive of these tall, bushy plants. Small branches extend alternately from either side of main branches (in a single plane).

**ABUNDANCE & DISTRIBUTION:** Common to occasional Florida, Bahamas, Caribbean.

**HABITAT & BEHAVIOR:** Grow in most marine environments from shallow to moderate depths. Attach to nearly any hard substrate.

**NOTE:** Visual identification probable, positive identification requires laboratory examination of collected specimen.

## WHITE MERMAID'S WINE GLASS
*Acetabularia crenulata*
PHYLUM:
Chlorophyta
**Green Algae**

SIZE: Height
³/₄ - 3¹/₄ in.
Cap Diameter
¹/₄ - ³/₄ in.
DEPTH: 3 - 20 ft.

## GREEN MERMAID'S WINE GLASS
*Acetabularia calyculus*
PHYLUM:
Chlorophyta
**Green Algae**

SIZE: Height
¹/₂ - 1¹/₂ in.
Cap Diameter
¹/₄ in.
DEPTH: 1 - 18 ft.

## PINK BUSH ALGA
*Wrangelia penicillata*
PHYLUM:
Rhodophyta
**Red Algae**

SIZE: 4 - 8 in.
DEPTH: 3 - 50 ft.

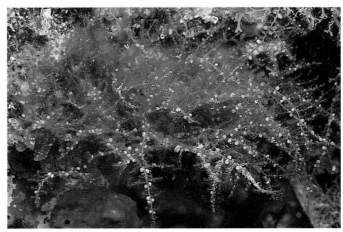

**VISUAL ID:** Several members of this genus cannot be distinguished visually and require laboratory examination for positive identification. In general their segments profusely branch dichotomously forming dense hemispherical domes attached by a single holdfast. Segments are tubular, smooth and relatively hard (heavily calcified) with flexible joints. Branch tips appear crosscut and have a central hole. Reddish to orangish and off-white.

**ABUNDANCE & DISTRIBUTION:** Common to occasional Florida, Bahamas, Caribbean.

**HABITAT & BEHAVIOR:** Generally inhabit protected areas of sand and rocks or rocky substrates, occasionally on shallow patch reefs. Attach to rocks and other hard substrates.

**VISUAL ID:** Grow in tangled, small clumps. Wide, dichotomously branched structures composed of rigid, stony, cylindrical segments and flexible joints. Segments light red to pink; joints white.

**ABUNDANCE & DISTRIBUTION:** Occasional Florida, Bahamas, Caribbean.

**HABITAT & BEHAVIOR:** Generally inhabit protected, somewhat shaded areas of reef. Often fill small cracks, nooks and depressions in rocky substrate.

**NOTE:** Visual identification probable, positive identification requires laboratory examination of collected specimen.

## TUBULAR THICKET ALGAE
*Galaxaura* sp.
PHYLUM:
Rhodophyta
**Red Algae**

SIZE: 4 - 6 in.
DEPTH: 3 - 40 ft.

## PINK SEGMENTED ALGA
*Jania adherens*
PHYLUM
Rhodophyta
**Red Algae**

SIZE: Height 1 - 2 in.
DEPTH: 0 - 60 ft.

**VISUAL ID:** Grow in tangled, small clumps. Randomly branched structures composed of stony, flat, thin segments. Flexible, obscure joints at forks of branches. Whitish with light red to pink tinting.

**ABUNDANCE & DISTRIBUTION:** Occasional Florida, Bahamas, Caribbean.

**HABITAT & BEHAVIOR:** Primarily inhabit reef crests and fore reefs. Generally in protected, somewhat shaded areas. May fill small cracks, nooks and depressions in rocky substrate.

---

**VISUAL ID:** Grow in tangled, small clumps formed of widely spaced, stony, thin, cylindrical, dichotomously forked branches. Flexible joints are obscure and rarely occur at forks. Whitish, often with light red to pink tinting.

**ABUNDANCE & DISTRIBUTION:** Occasional Florida, Bahamas, Caribbean.

**HABITAT & BEHAVIOR:** Often grow in shallow grass beds. Also inhabit reefs, generally in protected, somewhat shaded areas. May fill small cracks, nooks and depressions in rocky substrate.

**SIMILAR SPECIES:** *A. brasiliana* distinguished by pink color, somewhat flattened and more tightly bunched branches. *A. fragilissima* distinguished by swollen segment ends and wide angle of dichotomous branching forming thickly tangled clumps.

---

**VISUAL ID:** Thin, hard, highly calcified encrustations overgrowing rocky, limestone substrates. Take on surface texture of substrate. Shades of pinkish gray.

**ABUNDANCE & DISTRIBUTION:** Abundant to common Florida Keys, Bahamas, Caribbean.

**HABITAT & BEHAVIOR:** Most common on subtidal to intertidal reef crests where it can cover huge areas. Often in areas of clustered small holes, bored by chitons, *Acanthochitona lata*, that feed on other algae. Very important reef building element, acting as a cement-like covering and adhesive that protects the structure from the destructive elements of strong surge and breaking waves.

### FLAT TWIG ALGA
*Amphiroa tribulus*
PHYLUM
Rhodophyta
**Red Algae**

SIZE: Height 1 - 4 in.
DEPTH: 0 - 40 ft.

### Y-TWIG ALGA
*Amphiroa rigida*
PHYLUM
Rhodophyta
**Red Algae**

SIZE: Height 3 - 6 in.
DEPTH: 0 - 60 ft.

### REEF CEMENT
*Porolithon*
*pachydermum*
PHYLUM:
Rhodophyta
**Red Algae**

SIZE: N/A
DEPTH: 0 - 30 ft.

235

# Red Algae

**VISUAL ID:** There are a number of species in several genera that generally form thin, brittle, highly calcified encrustations and rounded plates. Occasionally their outer edges extend outward from substrate. They are usually dark red to burgundy, violet, lavender or pink, often with thin white margins. May be quite fragile, especially along extended edges. Colonies are so individually variable in appearance, and yet similar to one another, that they cannot easily be distinguished visually. Positive identification requires laboratory examination that includes decalcification, sectioning and microscopic examination.

**ABUNDANCE & DISTRIBUTION:** Common Florida, Bahamas, Caribbean.

**HABITAT & BEHAVIOR:** Prefer shaded areas of most marine environments, attaching to and encrusting solid substrates. Often the predominate growth in cracks, crevices, and along the walls of caves and narrow canyons. On sloping substrates, extended outer edges often overlap in a shingle-like fashion.

## CRUSTOSE CORALLINE ALGAE

**PHYLUM:**
Rhodophyta
**Red Algae**

**SIZE:** Plates 1 - 18 in.
**DEPTH:** 0 - 130 plus ft.

**Green Halimeda sp.**

**VISUAL ID:** Thin, hard, highly calcified encrusting growth taking on contours of substrate much like a painted coating. Dark red to burgundy. Outer margins may not be tightly attached.

**ABUNDANCE & DISTRIBUTION:** Abundant to occasional Florida, Bahamas, Caribbean.

**HABITAT & BEHAVIOR:** Prefer shaded areas of most marine environments, attaching to and encrusting solid substrates. Often the predominate growth in cracks, crevices, and along the walls of caves, canyons and deep drop-offs.

**NOTE:** Visual genus identification probable, positive identification requires laboratory examination that includes decalcification, sectioning and microscopic examination.

---

**VISUAL ID:** Several visually indistinguishable species form thin, brittle, highly calcified encrustations on surfaces of many species of algae and Turtle Grass (pictured here on Sea Pearls [pg. 219]). Surface texture generally smooth, but occasionally covered with small, knobby, cobblestone-like, reproductive structures. Usually shades of grayish lavender. Species may be classified in *Titanoderma, Fosliella,* or *Melobesia.*

**ABUNDANCE & DISTRIBUTION:** Abundant to occasional Florida, Bahamas, Caribbean.

**HABITAT & BEHAVIOR:** Common in most marine environments.

---

**VISUAL ID:** A number of species in this phylum form fuzzy masses of filaments. Generally dark red to burgundy to reddish tan. These colonies are so individually variable in appearance, and yet similar to one another, that they cannot easily be distinguished visually. Positive identification requires laboratory examination of filaments.

**ABUNDANCE & DISTRIBUTION:** Common  Florida, Bahamas, Caribbean.

**HABITAT & BEHAVIOR:** Prefer sunlit areas of most marine environments. Often have no permanent holdfast and snag on branches of other plants and colonial organisms.

**NOTE:** Pictured specimen is possibly *Symploca hydnoides*

### BURGUNDY CRUST ALGAE
*Peyssonnelia* sp.
PHYLUM:
Rhodophyta
**Red Algae**

SIZE: 1 - 3 ft.
DEPTH: 0 - 660 ft.

### LAVENDER CRUST ALGAE

PHYLUM:
Rhodophyta
**Red Algae**

SIZE: Diameter ½ - 2 in.
DEPTH: 0 - 100 ft.

### FUZZ BALL ALGA

PHYLUM:
Cyanophyta
**Blue-green Algae**

SIZE: 1 - 3 in.
DEPTH: 0 - 80 plus ft.

# INDEX

# PERSONAL RECORD OF FISH SIGHTINGS

## 1. FIRE & LACE CORALS

| No. | Name | Page | Date | Location | Notes |
|---|---|---|---|---|---|
| | Branching Fire Coral<br>*Millepora alcicornis* | 17 | | | |
| | Blade Fire Coral<br>*Millepora complanata* | 19 | | | |
| | Box Fire Coral<br>*Millepora squarrosa* | 19 | | | |
| | Rose Lace Coral<br>*Stylaster roseus* | 21 | | | |

## 2. GORGONIANS, TELESTACEANS & SOFT CORALS

| | | | | | |
|---|---|---|---|---|---|
| | Corky Sea Finger<br>*Briareum asbestinum* | 27 | | | |
| | Encrusting Gorgonian<br>*Erythropodium caribaeorum* | 29 | | | |
| | Black Sea Rod<br>*Plexaura homomalla* | 29 | | | |
| | Bent Sea Rod<br>*Plexaura flexuosa* | 31 | | | |
| | Porous Sea Rods<br>*Pseudoplexaura sp.* | 33 | | | |
| | Knobby Sea Rods<br>*Eunicea sp.* | 35 | | | |
| | Swollen-Knob Candelabrum<br>*Eunicea mammosa* | 35 | | | |
| | Shelf-Knob Sea Rod<br>*Eunicea succinea* | 37 | | | |
| | Warty Sea Rod<br>*Eunicea calyculata* | 39 | | | |
| | Doughnut Sea Rod<br>*Eunicea fusca* | 39 | | | |
| | Slit-Pore Sea Rods<br>*Plexaurella sp.* | 41 | | | |
| | Giant Slit-Pore Sea Rod<br>*Plexaurella nutans* | 43 | | | |
| | Spiny Sea Fan<br>*Muricea muricata* | 43 | | | |
| | Long Spine Sea Fan<br>*Muricea pinnata* | 45 | | | |
| | Orange Spiny Sea Rod<br>*Muricea elongata* | 47 | | | |
| | Delicate Spiny Sea Rod<br>*Muricea laxa* | 47 | | | |
| | Rough Sea Plume<br>*Muriceopsis flavida* | 49 | | | |
| | Sea Plumes<br>*Pseudopterogorgia sp.* | 51 | | | |
| | Slimy Sea Plume<br>*Pseudopterogorgia americana* | 51 | | | |
| | Bipinnate Sea Plume<br>*Pseudopterogorgia bipinnata* | 53 | | | |
| | Yellow Sea Whip<br>*Pterogorgia citrina* | 53 | | | |
| | Grooved-Blade Sea Whip<br>*Pterogorgia guadalupensis* | 55 | | | |
| | Angular Sea Whip<br>*Pterogorgia anceps* | 57 | | | |
| | Common Sea Fan<br>*Gorgonia ventalina* | 57 | | | |

| No. | Name | Page | Date | Location | Notes |
|---|---|---|---|---|---|
| | Venus Sea Fan<br>*Gorgonia ventalina* | 59 | | | |
| | Wide-Mesh Sea Fan<br>*Gorgonia mariae* | 61 | | | |
| | Deepwater Sea Fan<br>*Iciligorgia schrammi* | 61 | | | |
| | Colorful Sea Rod<br>*Diodogorgia nodulifera* | 63 | | | |
| | Brilliant Sea Fingers<br>*Titanideum frauenfeldii* | 65 | | | |
| | Red Polyp Octocoral<br>*Swiftia exserta* | 65 | | | |
| | Devil's Sea Whip<br>*Ellisella barbadensis* | 67 | | | |
| | Long Sea Whip<br>*Ellisella elongata* | 69 | | | |
| | Orange Deep Water Fan<br>*Nicella goreaui* | 69 | | | |
| | Bushy Sea Whip<br>*Nicella schmitti* | 71 | | | |
| | Colorful Sea Whip<br>*Leptogorgia virgulata* | 73 | | | |
| | Regal Sea Fan<br>*Leptogorgia hebes* | 75 | | | |
| | Carmine Sea Spray<br>*Leptogorgia miniata* | 75 | | | |
| | Pinnate Spiny Sea Fan<br>*Muricea pendula* | 77 | | | |
| | White Eye Sea Spray<br>*Thesea nivea* | 79 | | | |
| | Golden Sea Spray<br>*Heterogorgia uatumani* | 81 | | | |
| | Rigid Red Telesto<br>*Stereotelesto corallina* | 81 | | | |
| | White Telesto<br>*Carijoa riisei* | 83 | | | |
| | Orange Telesto<br>*Telesto fruticulosa* | 83 | | | |
| | Pastel Soft Coral<br>*Neospongodes portoricensis* | 85 | | | |

### 3. STONY CORALS

| No. | Name | Page | Date | Location | Notes |
|---|---|---|---|---|---|
| | Staghorn Coral<br>*Acropora cervicornis* | 91 | | | |
| | Fused Staghorn<br>*Acropora prolifera* | 91 | | | |
| | Elkhorn Coral<br>*Acropora palmata* | 93 | | | |
| | Blue Crust Coral<br>*Porites branneri* | 93 | | | |
| | Finger Coral<br>*Porites porites* | 95 | | | |
| | Pillar Coral<br>*Dendrogyra cylindrus* | 97 | | | |
| | Tube Coral<br>*Cladocora arbuscula* | 99 | | | |
| | Robust Ivory Tree Coral<br>*Oculina robusta* | 99 | | | |
| | Delicate Ivory Bush Coral<br>*Oculina tenella* | 101 | | | |
| | Diffuse Ivory Bush Coral<br>*Oculina diffusa* | 101 | | | |
| | Large Ivory Coral<br>*Oculina varicosa* | 103 | | | |